GW00399926

2439	Eser:	Niyazi Mısri Tasavvufi Şiirleri
	Yazar:	Niyazi Mısri
	Yayıncı	Kopernik, Inc. (Kopernik Publishing House)
	Ülke:	İngilizce

THE ARCHITECT
OF
LOVE

Sufi Poems by
NİYAZİ MISRI

Translated by Ersin Balcı

kopernik

NİYAZİ MISRİ, is one of the most prominent Anatolian sufis of the 17th century and is, to this day, a venerated sufi master whose renown reaches far beyond Anatolia. He was a Khalwati sufi master who is especially well-known for his beautiful, spiritually energizing sufi poems which have been widely read in Turkish sufi circles for centuries. He also wrote in the form of prose, most of which are short treatises written mostly under the great influence of Muhyiddin ibn Arabi, the renowned 12th-13th century Andalusian sufi.

ERSİN BALCI, the translator of *The Architect of Love - Sufi Poems by Niyazi Mısri*, was born in 1965 in Düzce, Turkey. He studied philosophy at the Middle East Technical University, Ankara. He has translated the *Fusus al-Hikam* by Muhyiddin ibn Arabi and *The Way of Muhammad* by Abdalqadir as-Sufi into Turkish. He has also translated *The Journey to the Beloved - Sufi Poems by Yunus Emre and Gather Sunlight for Me: A Selection of Modern Turkish Poetry* into English. He is the author of *Kendi Kitabını Oku (Read Your Own Book)*, a book on sufism, which he is now translating into English.

First published by Kopernik Inc.
®Ersin Balcı 2019

Editor-in-Chief: Abdülkadir Özkan
Advisor: Prof. Halil Berktay
Series Editor: Dr. Yaşar Çolak
Director: Dr. Cengiz Şişman
Translated by: Ersin Balcı
Design: Ali Kaya
Application: Sinopsis

Kopernik Publishing House
Kopernik Inc.
108 Olde Towne Avenue Unit: 308 Gaithersburg Maryland 20877 - USA
www.kopernikpublishing.com

Certification no: 35175
ISBN: 978-605-69195-7-2
First Edition: August 2019

Printed in ISTANBUL
Bilnet Matbaacılık - 42716

ISTANBUL - LONDON - NEW YORK – WASHINGTON DC

THE ARCHITECT
OF
LOVE

Sufi Poems by
NİYAZİ MISRI

Translated by Ersin Balcı

kopernik

CONTENTS

PREFACE

True spiritual Masters are like rivers, each with their own uniquely pure, sweet water, nourished by the highest peaks. Although one may see them flowing on the surface, mostly, they are underground rivers, making it hard to access them. But, if one finds a way to access a true spiritual Master, you will very soon realize that he is, amazingly, a door, a passageway to the deepest realities of existence, a healing for wounded hearts, and a secure harbor within the unending turmoils of life.

With that encounter with a true spiritual Master, if you let it happen, a vibrant, marvellous, and intoxicating dance of the heart begins which will take you to the unexpected beauties of your inner existence. I hope, this book, *The Architect of Love*, which includes a selection of fifty English-translated poems, will open a way for readers to experience such an encounter with the mighty spiritual presence of Niyazi Mısri, the great Turkish sufi Master, who lived in the 17th century Ottoman period.

Of course, every translation project is a challenge for the translator; and, this is especially true when you are translating poems by a sufi Master, as one needs to keep one's eyes open for deeper and deeper meanings of the literal words. On the other hand, in an meticulous effort to be able to convey the peerless fragrance of his spirituality in English, I tried hard to maintain both the original meaning of the poems and their poetic taste. Yet, despite these challenges, translating his wonderful poems has been a marvellous adventure for me from the very beginning to the very end.

At this point, for helping me to finalize this adventure of mine, I would like to offer my ardent thanks to Amy Sevil, Margret Sönmez, and Tim Thurston who wholeheartedly did their best in language editing of the manuscripts; and, I have to acknowledge that without their painstaking efforts, this graceful translation of poems would have never been accomplished.

INTRODUCTION

Niyazi Mısri (1618-1694) is one of the most prominent Anatolian sufis of the 17th century and is, to this day, a venerated sufi master whose renown reaches far beyond Anatolia. He was a khalifa of Khalwati Sheikh Ümmi Sinan of Elmalı, and later he established an order known as the Mısriyya, a synthesis of Qadiriyya and Khalwatiyya. Niyazi Mısri is especially well-known for his beautiful, spiritually energizing sufi poems which have been widely read in Turkish sufi circles for centuries.

The Life of Niyazi Mısri

Although he is known as Niyazi Mısri, his real name is Muhammed, "Niyazi" and "Mısri" being only the pen names he used in his poems. He was born on March 9, 1618, in Malatya, a city in eastern Anatolia. His father, Soğancızade Ali Çelebi, a Naqshbandi sufi, was among the notables of the city.

After completing elementary school, he continued his education by attending courses on religious sciences from the notable religious scholars of Malatya. In those early years, he became a disciple of Hüseyin Efendi, a Khalwati sufi master.

He himself relates: "In my adolescence, I had in my heart the desire to know the sufi way. In the beginning, being opposed to them, I did not participate in their gatherings. But later on, day by day my aspiration increased with the blessing of their discourses. Finally, I became a disciple of a Khalwati sufi master."

After his Master passed away, leaving Malatya to find a spiritual guide and to improve himself in religious sciences, he went to Diyarbakır and Mardin, staying one year in each city, where he attended lectures of theology and logic. Then, he went to Cairo, in 1640, where he stayed three years. There, he became a disciple of a Qadiri sufi master, Sheikh İbrahim, and while attending the religious lectures given in the al-Azhar Mosque during the daytime, he continued his spiritual training in the sufi lodge during the nights. However, one day, his Master said: "You have to give up outward knowledge if you want the knowledge of the Way be open to you." That night, he went to sleep with a great sorrow in his heart, and in a dream, he saw the venerable sufi master Sheikh Abdulqadir Jilani, the founder of Qadiriyya. Niyazi Mısri relates that dream:

"I saw myself in a big city as a man in the service of the Sultan. This Sultan, who had a palace with a large courtyard, was Abdulqadir Jilani. There, he was performing ablution among a crowded group of his attendants. I was standing by him, anxious that he would rebuke me, but I was unable to leave. He saw and called out to me: 'O, sufi!' I turned towards him at once and stood before him. He ordered one of his servants to bring him a pouch of coins. After the servant had taken some steps, he called him back, saying, 'I will give him the pouch myself.' He put his hand into his pocket and brought out a pouch and gave it to me. When I opened it before him, I saw that there were silver coins in it, and within the pouch, there was another one, which I opened, too. In this one, there were gold coins. I asked him: 'What are the meanings of these two pouches?' He replied: 'The silver coins are outward knowledge; learn and act upon it. The gold coins are knowledge of the Way which you can only attain through one who is predestined for you,' adding, 'Your Guide is not in this city.' I woke up with relief and a joy that I cannot describe."

Having seen this dream, Niyazi Mısri, taking permission from his Master, set out on a journey to find the true Guide indicated by Abdulqadir Jilani. For several years he wandered through Egypt, Syria and Anatolia. When he was in Bursa, he saw another dream. In that dream, a tinsmith was making cups in a shop crowded with customers. Mısri came to that shop to have his ablution pitcher tinned, he handed it to the tinsmith who took it and said, "The outside can be tinned by anyone, the skill is tinning them inside." Then, he split the pitcher in two and tinned both the outside and the inside; and, joining the pieces, he gave it back.

Niyazi Mısri intuitively concluded that this tinsmith was the Guide he had been seeking. So, he continued on his journey until he came to Uşak where he stayed as a guest in the sufi lodge of Mehmed Efendi, one of the khalifas of Yusuf Sinan Ümmi, a Khalwati Sheikh from Elmalı. There, he deeply felt in his heart that the Guide he had been seeking was none but Ümmi Sinan. Soon it was heard that Ümmi Sinan was on the way to Uşak to pay a visit. With great joy, Sheikh Mehmed Efendi and his followers set out to welcome Ümmi Sinan, Niyazi Mısri with them. They welcomed him on the road, some miles away from Uşak. At nightfall, after dinner, Ümmi Sinan asked Mehmed Efendi: "Is there any dervish with you whose name is Muhammed Niyazi?" Mehmed Efendi replied: "Yes, my Master, he is with us." Then, Ümmi Sinan said to Niyazi Mısri: "That tinsmith was an intriguing person, wasn't he?" — pointing out that he himself was the Guide he had been seeking for four years of yearning.

Niyazi Mısri writes about this meeting with Ümmi Sinan, his beloved spiritual Master: "I had set out on the journey to find him. In the cities of Arab countries and Anatolia, I attended many a sufi masters' discourses. Eventually, I attained the service of Ümmi Sinan of Elmalı, who is the light of my eye and the remedy for my heart. I have found the cure for my heart in the honour of being in his service. What Abdulqadir Jilani had pointed out with his blessed breath in my dream came true."

Niyazi Mısri went to Elmalı where he stayed in the service of Ümmi Sinan from 1647 to 1656. After nine years of spiritual training, when he was 40 years old, Ümmi Sinan gave Niyazi Mısri a *khilafat-namah* and sent him to Uşak to guide people on the spiritual path. While he was making preparations for moving to Uşak, some friends, having obtained Ümmi Sinan's permission, asked him to make a religious speech to the people of Elmalı in the mosque. When he sat down to deliver the sermon, he forgot all he knew and did not know what to say. Ümmi Sinan who was among the audience exclaimed: "Speak, O Mısri Efendi; from now on, do not be silent, ever speak!" He could then speak and gave a beautiful speech on divine realities. Niyazi Mısri, mentioning this event later, said: "With this permission and spiritual help of my Master we are still talking, for us there is nothing to fear."

After Niyazi Mısri set out on his journey to Uşak, some people asked Ümmi Sinan why he had sent him to Uşak instead of a big city like Bursa, upon which he answered: "You will see that our dervish Mısri will be contained in neither

Uşak nor Bursa, nor any other land. He will be a well-known spiritual master, a high ranked one, and one among the perfected ones."

While Niyazi Mısri was staying in Uşak, Mehmed Efendi wanted him to go to Çal, a small town in Afyon, where he stayed for a short period of time, and then to Kütahya, where he stayed nearly one year, carrying about his duty of spiritual guidance of people. In 1658, after the passing away of his beloved Master, Ümmi Sinan, he left Kütahya and moved to Bursa, where he became a widely known and respected sufi master. Thus, what Ümmi Sinan said about him years before came true.

◆ ◆ ◆

The 17th century Ottoman period in which Niyazi Mısri lived was full of social and political turmoil. This was a time when the Ottoman Empire was in decline after reaching its peak in the 16th century. Weakness and misconduct in state administration, the deterioration of social and political institutions, outbreaks of Jelali rebellions in rural Anatolia, widely threatening social security and stability, and remarkable military defeats against European armies were the events that marked the century. The same period also saw the rise of the religious movement of Kadızadelis, a group of salafi-oriented mosque preachers who terrorized the whole society—especially the sufis—throughout the century with their ignorant bigotry. In 1666, with their influence on the state governors, they managed to make the two sufi rituals of *dawran* and *sama* prohibited with the claim that they were innovated practices contrary to Islam. Sufi lodges were therefore closed until 1674. These were very trying years as sufi lodges were attacked and sometimes destroyed, and adherents to sufi orders were severely assaulted and beaten. A few sufi masters, Niyazi

Mısri being one of them, disobeyed the prohibition and let their disciples perform *dawran* and *sama* in their sufi lodges, but this was not without its consequences, as there were times when Niyazi Mısri could not even leave his house because of the violent assaults by Kadızadeli mobs. Day by day, the number of his opponents and enemies increased as he was an outspoken man, never refraining from bitterly criticizing the bigotry of the Kadızadelis, the political authorities, and even the Sultan himself. This hostile environment eventually brought about the exile years of Niyazi Mısri — once to the isle of Rhodes and twice to the isle of Lemnos.

To give a little context for the reader, it's noteworthy to mention that he was not an exception in being exiled as a sufi master by state authorities, since in the time he lived other sufi masters were also exiled, İsmail Ankaravi, the renowned Mawlawi sufi master who wrote a seven volume of commentary on *Masnawi* by Mevlana Celaleddin Rumi, was one of them. Ankaravi relates about his exile, picturing the atmosphere of terror caused by Kadizadelis: "While I, the poor, was occupied with guiding and advising people in our home town, some people of malice, casting lies and aspersions, caused me to be exiled, being blamed with misconduct. They even tried to kill me more than once. Yet, my Lord saved me from their tricks and traps."

◆◆◆

In 1675, on critically speaking out against the corruption and misuse of state authorities, Niyazi Mısri was sentenced to exile for the first time and sent to Rhodes where he stayed for nearly nine months. Then, he returned to Bursa upon the lifting of the sentence by the Sultan.

One year later, in 1677, the religious authorities blamed him for his speech on some intricate issues of sufi doctrine claiming his words were contrary to orthodox religious creed, after which he was sentenced to exile, this time, to Lemnos, for two years. However, although his sentence is over, rather than returning back, he preferred staying there. After living 15 more years in Lemnos, upon the request of Grand Vizier Köprülüzade Mustafa Paşa, he returned to Bursa, in 1692.

Niyazi Mısri's last exile came when, in 1693, Sultan Ahmed II invited him to join a military campaign against Austrians to raise the morale of soldiers as a venerable sufi master. On his way to Edirne, where the army was gathering for the campaign, people began to rally around him to join him for the campaign; and, on his arrival in Edirne, as he went straight to the Selimiye Mosque, there he found a large crowd of locals and soldiers who had gathered to welcome him. This great show of ardor for Niyazi Mısri worried some government authorities, as there were also rumors among people that Niyazi Mısri was going to inform on the treacherous government officers to the Sultan himself. They, fueling the Sultan with the fear that such a gathering of people might turn into a rebellious movement against the state, persuaded him to exile Niyazi Mısri to Lemnos for a second time. This was an exile of no return as he passed away in the year of 1694, at the age of 78. His tomb remains there, in Lemnos, to this day.

Influential Figures on Niyazi Mısri's Poetry and Thought

Niyazi Mısri not only had a formal madrasa education, but also had long journeys in which he visited, stayed, and lived in various cities like Cairo, Istanbul, and Bursa which had well-established sufi life and culture. Niyazi Mısri was very much a part of a dynamic interactive sufi environment which enabled him to enrich his spiritual experience and knowledge. Thus, there is no wonder that this well-educated man with a sophisticated knowledge of Islam and sufism was influenced by various sufi writers and poets. Although it's maybe unwise to narrow down such a rich sphere of influence to a few people, there are some obvious examples which should not go unmentioned.

In his poetry, Niyazi Mısri was explicitly influenced by the poems of Yunus Emre, the well-known 14th century Anatolian sufi poet. He himself, acknowledges this in one of his poems, saying,

It is Yunus speaking
Through the tongue of Niyazi;
As everyone is in need of a soul,
Yunus is the soul for me.

In fact, this influence is sometimes so explicit that in some of his poems, we come across expressions which are almost the same as those used by Yunus Emre himself.

It's also known that, Niyazi Mısri, had great fondness for Mawlaviyya and Mawlana Jalaluddin Rumi for whom he wrote an Arabic poem, praising him. As he delighted by the impressive spiritual aura of Mawlawiyya, he sometimes paid visits to the Mawlavi Sufi lodge in Bursa, where he would listen to the reed-flute in tears. Sometimes he also had Mehmed Dede, the Mawlawi Sheikh of Bursa, read some couplets from the *Masnawi* of Rumi and explained their meaning to him, telling which stations they indicate.

At the same time, Niyazi Mısri was a great admirer of Muhyiddin ibn Arabi, the renowned 12th-13th century Andalusian sufi, who visited Anatolia three times in the first quarter of the 13th century, staying in Konya and Malatya for six years in total. He exerted, especially through his stepson Sadreddin Konevi, a very deep and centuries-long lasting impact on Anatolian sufis, Niyazi Mısri being one of them. In one of his poems, in which he praises the book *Waridat* and its author, Sheikh Bedreddin, an 14th-15th century Anatolian sufi, he also speaks highly of Muhyiddin ibn Arabi, and of his renowned book *Fusus al-Hikam*, saying:

> *The knowledge of* Fusus *quenchs all the fires of the hell,*
> W aridat *is the flowers growing in place of them.*

> *Muhyiddin and Bedreddin have revived the religion,*
> *Niyazi, the ocean is* Fusus, *the rivers of which are* W aridat.

Poems and Poetic Style of Niyazi Mısri

After the adoption of Islam by Turkish peoples, Anatolian Turkish literature developed in two main genres of poetical style. On the one hand, there was folk poetry with its roots in pre-Islamic Turkish culture, and on the other, there was *divan* poetry, borrowed from Persian and Arabic cultures, the homelands of the Islamic tradition. While the former was popular mostly among uneducated rural people, the latter was popular mostly among the urban educated. Anatolian Turkish sufis, with their wish to reach to both of these audiences, mostly wrote in a poetical style which blended both *divan* and folk poetry, a style which culminated in Yunus Emre.

This blend of styles can be seen in the work of Niyazi Mısri. A large number of his poems are written in *aruz* prosody and in the poetic form of *ghazal*, following the style of *divan* poetry, but some of his poems are written in syllabic prosody, following the Turkish folk poetic tradition. Whilst using Arabic and Persian words and phrases to express necessary religious sufi terminology and concepts, the plain language of common people can easily be discerned in his poems as well. He conveys the meaning he intends in a straightforward manner without giving much importance to the formal aspects of poetry, but within this simplicity is a strong voice — his poems are impassioned, powerful and motivational and are written in a gnostic and ecstatic manner.

Niyazi Mısri's sufi poems are compiled in *Divan-ı İlahiyyat*, the most well-known work of Niyazi Mısri, which is also considered as being a manual for those on the sufi path. Although almost all the poems in the book are in Turkish, there are also some Arabic-written poems. There are many extant manuscript copies of the *Divan*, the most reliable and earliest of which is the one inscribed by Mahmud Efendi, one of the khalifas of Niyazi Mısri, in Lemnos, in 1699. The English-translated poems of the present book, *The Architect of Love*, were selected from the poems included in this reliable manuscript of 187 poems.

Niyazi Mısri's poems were highly esteemed in sufi circles and seen worthy of detailed commentary. Muhammed Nur'ul Arabi, the founder of the third epoch of Malamiyya, wrote a book of commentary, explaining almost all his poems. Turkish sufis such as İsmail Hakkı Bursevi, Haririzade Kemaleddin Efendi, Ali Urfi Efendi, Selim Baba, Hasan Sezayi Efendi, Mustafa Aczi Ağa, and Hüseyin Vassaf were amongst those who also wrote commentaries on some of his poems. At the same time as being widely read in Turkish sufi circles for centuries, more than 100 of his poems have been rendered into popular sufi songs. Among the composers who have set his poems to music are famous Ottoman-Turkish musicians like Itri, Dede Efendi, Hafiz Post, Ali Şirugani, Mustafa Anber Ağa, Mehmed Zaifi Efendi, Zekai Dede and Saadettin Arel.

Sufi Symbolism in Niyazi Mısri's Poems

To understand the spiritual context of Niyazi Mısri's poems in depth, one needs to be acquainted with the symbolic language he extensively uses, following the long-standing sufi poetry tradition which began to flourish in the 8th century.

The reason for the use of symbolic language by sufis is due to the experiential nature of their spiritual journey; it is something that can only be 'tasted' and is therefore difficult to express in words. When they communicate their spiritual experiences to others, they therefore have to use metaphors and symbols to indicate that which lies beyond.

Sufism is a doctrine whose central concern is God and it states that the only real being in existence is none but Him. In this sense, all others, including man, have only a shadow-reality. In this world, only man can awaken to this fact and can be able to return to the Source to realise himself in a state of unification with God. This is why sufis focus on striving to overcome their separation from God, yearning for a unification with Him where the truth of their existence lies; their former state just being one of false consciousness. So, for sufis the relation of man with God becomes a relation of a lover with his Beloved. In order to express their yearning for God and a state of unification with Him, they developed a rich symbolic and metaphorical language, using the imagery of earthly love used in classical Arabic and Persian poetry.

In the very heart of this imagery lies the story of *Laila and Majnun*, a classic story of love, based on a semi-historical 7th century Arab story. Majnun, the love-crazed lover of Laila, symbolizes one who is lost in Love for God. Sufis describe God the Beloved as a female figure because in Arabic, God's Essential Reality (*Dhat*) is grammatically feminine in gender and they ascribe Him a Face of Beauty, following the Koranic verse: "Wherever you turn, there is the Face of Allah" [the Koran, 2:115]. Hence comes a bouquet of symbolic imagery, borrowed from classical poetry, relating to Her Beauty, or *Jamal*, a Name ascribed to God in the Koran.

Dark curls and tresses —Laila means 'night' referring to her dark hair— both refer to the unknown, unattainable Essence and to the veil of *Jalal* — that is the whole creation which veils the Beauty of God. So, in the latter sense, tresses symbolize the shadow-reality of the manifoldness of creation, veiling the Oneness of God. Therefore, to be bewitched by dark tresses —which hinders seeing the Facial Beauty of the Beloved— implies ignorance and unbelief. The lips of the Beloved represent the words of the Beloved or Divine Life; her cheek stands for the manifestation of the lights of the self-manifestation of God; her mole, or beauty-spot symbolizes the indivisible Oneness of God and the down on Her cheek, God's attribute of Majesty and Greatness.

◆ ◆ ◆

Sufi poets also frequently use the imagery of wine and drunkenness. This symbolism, too, has its roots in the Koran: "And their Lord shall offer them pure wine" [the Koran, 76:12]. These words are part of God's depictions of Heavenly life in the hereafter. As sufis conceive Heaven as the nearness to God both in this world and in the hereafter, they interpret the pure wine mentioned in this verse as a metaphor for the spiritual ecstasy of Divine Love experienced in union with God. Hence comes another bouquet of symbolic imagery, again borrowed from classical poetry, relating to the spiritual ecstasy of Divine Love. First, the Cup in which the Wine is served symbolizes the heart of the Perfect Guide, being the treasure of Divine Love. And the Cup, from which the Wine is sipped, symbolizes the Heart of the Lover, thirsty for delightfully intoxicating Divine Love. Secondly, the Cup-bearer in this context is no one but the spiritual Guide who incites sparks of Divine Love in the hearts of the Lovers. Finally, the Tavern where frequenters drink wine, make merry, and get drunk is symbolic of where Lovers of God stay in the presence of their spiritual Guide, from whom Divine Love flows abundantly to fill their hearts.

◆ ◆ ◆

Another set of imagery commonly used by sufi poets to depict the relation of lover to the Beloved is that of the nightingale and the rose. In classical poetry, the nightingale is in love with the rose, for whom he sings his love and wails because of his yearning for his beloved. In sufi poetry, the nightingale comes to symbolize the Lover of God, and the rose, God the Beloved. Additionally, there is the rose garden, which stands for the Oneness of God where the multiplicity of creation is veiled.

Other imagery, which takes the love relation a step further, is the relation of a moth to the flame of the candle. Here, the lover is the moth, who is attracted to the flame of the candle, the beloved. This attraction ultimately ends with the moth burning, and therefore becoming one with the flame itself. Therefore, in sufi poetry, this imagery comes to symbolize the annihilation of the seeker within the Absolute Beauty of God.

◆ ◆ ◆

Sufi poets also uses the dichotomic relation between the Ocean and the drop as an imagery, in which drop stands for the individual existence of man, whereas Ocean stands for the Unity of God, the only Being beyond the shadow reality of the universe. The drop is the false consciousness of the self, surmising that it has a separate existence in itself, an existence other than God — but, when it merges into the Ocean, it becomes unified with it.

The ocean/drop dichotomy is also used by sufi poets to represent the dichotomy of macrocosmos/microcosmos. While in terms of his outer reality man is just a drop in the ocean, in terms of his inner reality, there is an ocean within that drop as man is the epitome of the universe, gathering together in himself all the dispersed realities of it.

In the imagery of Ocean, the dichotomy of wave/Ocean is also widely used. Here, while the Ocean represents the Absolute Being of God, the waves of the Ocean stand for the becoming of the world of manifoldness which has no existence in itself, being only the self-manifestation of the Absolute Being.

◆◆◆

As well as this common imagery, Niyazi Mısri mentions Jesus Christ, Mahdi, and Dajjal in their symbolic meanings in his poems. From a sufi perspective, which establishes a correspondence between the microcosmos and the macrocosmos, 'doomsday' corresponds to the death of the ego or "dying before death" which is the only way to be born into eternal life. What will happen at the end of the times will surely happen in the very end of one's Inner Journey. In this sense, Jesus Christ, Mahdi, and Dajjal correspond inner states or stations one will pass through during one's Inner Journey.

The appearance of Dajjal is known to be one of the major signs of the end of the times. In *The Feasts of Wisdom*, Niyazi Mısri, explaining the inward meaning of Dajjal, says that Dajjal's coming out is the emergence of evil attributes in the soul which hinders man from seeing divine realities.

As to the killing of Dajjal by Jesus Christ, Niyazi Mısri explains it in *The Feasts of Wisdom* as the following: "The killing of Dajjal by Christ means the annulment of the sovereignty of Dajjal. Just as Sadruddin Qunawi says: 'Dajjal is the place of manifestation of the reality of this world. It is for this reason that he is blind in the right eye, that is, he cannot perceive God. And Jesus Christ is the place of manifestation of the reality of hereafter.'"

And, as to Mahdi, Niyazi Mısri says: "The appearance of Mahdi is the manifestation of the Universal Intellect and Supreme Spirit, which is breathed only into the elect. The verse, "He breathed into him of His Spirit," [the Koran, 32:9] indicates this. The Perfect Guide, being the vicegerent of God, breathes that Spirit into the seeker."

Other Works by Niyazi Mısri

Other than his poems compiled in *Divan-ı İlahiyyat*, Niyazi Mısri has more than 30 sufi works written in prose, most of which are short treatises on different sufi topics. Although most of them are in Turkish, some of them were written in Arabic.

Mawaaid al-Irfaan (The Feasts of Wisdom) is the last work of Niyazi Mısri and is one of the most prominent works by him. The book, written in Arabic, consists of 71 short chapters. It includes his admonitions for the seekers of God, information on states to be experienced throughout the inner journey, and explanations on the inner meanings of Koranic verses.

Risale-i Es'ile ve Ecvibe-i Mutasavvufane is a treatise which explains some sufi terminology and which explains how the beliefs of the *ahl-i sunnah* and those of the sufis coincide. It's written in question and answer form. It's one of the most widely read works of Niyazi Mısri.

Vahdetname. A treatise on the Oneness of Being which includes verses and prophetic sayings, and Turkish, Arabic and Persian couplets on the degrees of faith and the goal of creation.

Şerh-i Nutk-ı Yunus Emre is a commentary on a well-known symbolic poem by Yunus Emre, *"Çıktım erik dalına anda yedim üzümü / Bostan ıssı kakıyıp der ne yersin kozumu."*

Other short works by Niyazi Mısri are:

Risale-i Devriyye, Risale-i Hızriyye, Risale-i Tevhid, Risale-i Eşratü's-Saat, Tabirname, Risale-i Arşiyye, Risale-i İade, Risale-i Nokta, Risale fi Devran-ı Sofiye, Şerh-i Esmaü'l-Hüsna, Risale-i Nefise, Risale-i Hasanayn, Tefsir-i Fatihatü'l Kitab, Tesbi-i Kaside-i Bürde, Mecalis, Mecmua-i Kelimat-ı Kudsiye, and *Etvar-ı Seb'a.*

THE ARCHITECT

OF

LOVE

1

Ey gönül gel gayrıdan geç aşka eyle iktidâ
Zümre-i ehl-i hakîkat am kılmş muktedâ

Abandon, O Heart, all else, and follow Love;
The People of Truth have ever followed Love.

Love precedes all that exists and is known,
No beginning could they find for Love.

After all is perished, Love goes on,
Thus they said: There is no end for Love.

Dear God, let Your help be my companion
And never separate my Heart from Your Love.

Remove from my Heart the desire
For that which is other than Your Love;
In both worlds, my intimate
Make Your Love.

For the Lover, hell is heaven — with Love,
For the Lover, heaven is hell — without Love.

O Niyazi, if you are seeking a Guide
On this Path, follow Love;
For all the Prophets and Friends of God,
The Guide has ever been Love.

2

Zehî kenz-i hafî k'andan gelir her var olur peydâ
Gehî zulmet zuhûr eder gehî envâr olur peydâ

What a wonder is the Hidden Treasure
Whence comes every single thing
And appears manifest;
Now darkness, now lights appear manifest.

With its waves endless,
What a wonder is the Ocean of Oneness!
Whence comes this world of manifoldness
Which cannot choose but appear manifest.

What wondrous magic it is
That from this Face others are seen!
Yet there is nought but this Face,
Singly comes the Beloved and appears manifest.

Every single essence, seeing Your Face,
Circles the Candle, that is, Your Beauty;
So do the spheres; seeing It, they circle,
Whereupon cycles appear manifest.

A hundred thousand souls are conveyed
Every day to the land of non-existence,
Whence come also a hundred thousand others
So as to prosper and appear manifest.

Imaginations of the outer towards the inner,
Manifestations of the inner towards the outer;
At every instant gifts, one to another,
Appear manifest.

Through the cycle of the heavens, there come
Prophets and Messengers one after another;
Now the believer, now the unbeliever
Appear manifest.

Whenever He unfolds Himself
In the Palace, that is, the Innermost Secret,
Within this world of outward forms
Dealings appear manifest.

There is no finitude for His Essence,
There is no end to His creation;
From each of His Names,
Comes a task and appears manifest.

He ever unfolds Himself
Now through His Beauty, now through His Majesty;
The one results in Heaven, and from the other,
Hell appears manifest.

Whenever His Beauty appears,
Instantly His Majesty overtakes It;
Whenever a rose blooms, on it,
You see thorns appear manifest.

Due to this secret, whenever
A Perfect Man appears in this world,
Some accept him, and in the others
Denial appears manifest.

Yet the Gnostic sees
Within Majesty His Beauty:
For him, in this land of thorns,
A Rose Garden appears manifest.

What Secret it is that
Two people behold the creation;
The one can see only the house,
To the other, the Owner appears manifest.

Its interior: the Ocean of Oneness,
Its exterior: the desert of manifoldness;
He who sees the without, sees that which is other,
In the within, the Beloved appears manifest.

He who delights in Oneness
Is delivered from duality;
Wherever he looks, there, O Niyazi,
The Beloved's Face appears manifest.

He sees how things emerge
From the Hidden Treasure,
And he knows, from each outward form,
How secrets appear manifest.

3

Ey gönül gel ağlama zâri zâri inleme
Pirden aldım haberi ol bî-nişân sendedir

O Heart, come, do not cry and moan,
Tears pouring from your eyes;
I have brought tidings from the Guide
That the Traceless is within you.

Within you is the Land of the Friend,
Within you blooms His Rose;
The nightingale-soul sings that
The cheerful Rose is within you.

Do not wander the lands and seas,
This Secret is to be found within you;
The Hidden Sultan who reigns
Over the body and the soul is within you.

If you have conceived of yourself,
And if you have known the soul and the body,
Nothing else is, O Heart,
The Sweetheart of the soul is within you.

This soul is the throne of the body,
The Sweetheart is the throne of the soul;
O Niyazi, without doubt,
That No-Place is within you.

4

Zahidâ sûret gözetme içeri gel câna bak
Vechi üzre gör ne yazmış defter-i Rahman'a bak

O ascetic, observe not the outward form,
Come inwards, the soul, behold;
See what has been written upon your Face,
The Book of the Merciful, behold.

On the pages of Her beauty
Has been written: *"Qul Hu wallah ..."*
If you believe it not, come and read,
The School of Gnosis, behold.

That Sweetheart, who, revealing
Her eyes, takes the Lover's life
And who, opening Her lips,
Breathes out Life, behold.

See a thousand Majnuns hanged
Upon each strand of Her tresses,
Those hundred thousand Moons
At the night of Her Mole, behold.

His face has been burnt
And darkened by the fires burning,
That Naked Point, stripped of
The robe of letters, behold.

The shahs are
All in constant servanthood to Him,
That Sultan, at the door of whom
The kings are servants, behold.

The world has been a Book
Expounding Her Beauty,
If you want to see its text, O Niyazi,
The form of Man, behold.

5

Bakıp cemâl-i yâre çağırıram dost dost
Dil oldu pâre pâre çağırıram dost dost

Gazing at the Beauty of the Beloved,
I call — Friend, O Friend!
My Heart has been torn apart,
I call — Friend, O Friend!

Brimmed with Your Love,
My piety in tatters,
Ever intoxicated,
I call — Friend, O Friend!

In the mosque and in the tavern,
In the mansion and in the ruin,
In the Kaaba and in the idol-temple,
I call — Friend, O Friend!

Cascading like running waters,
I sweep through the mountains,
At me marvels everyone,
I call — Friend, O Friend!

I have come to this world as a stranger,
I have become the Nightingale of the Rose,
Always piercing my breast,
I call — Friend, O Friend!

Giving up hankering after the world,
Taking my wings to Annihilation,
Ever flying with Love,
I call — Friend, O Friend!

What I seek is within the soul,
Within the soul and within the body;
Though I know that within me He is,
I call — Friend, O Friend!

Now I fall into the absolute,
Now into origin, now into creation;
Beholding the Truth in everything,
I call — Friend, O Friend!

Ever-present are Her Mole and Down
From and to eternity;
Caught with this incurable heartache,
I call — Friend, O Friend!

All that is seen is the Face of the Friend,
Never do I take my eyes from Him,
His Name is on my tongue, ever,
I call — Friend, O Friend!

Till my breath becomes ocean,
Till my cage is torn asunder,
Till my voice dies away,
I call — Friend, O Friend!

Revolving like the heavens,
Circling like the sun,
Enjoying the cycle of creation,
I call — Friend, O Friend!

I am neither on earth nor in heaven,
Neither dead nor alive am I,
Always and wherever I am,
I call — Friend, O Friend!

I have come from that Friend's Land,
Carrying with me the fragrance of His Rose,
Through Niyazi's tongue
I call — Friend, O Friend!

6

Hep güzeller arasında buldu hüsnün çün revâc
Cem olup uşşâk bir bir sana eyler ihtiyâc

Among the people of beauty,
Your Beauty has ever been in demand;
Lovers, gathering one by one,
From You they all helplessly demand.

What a kingdom of beauty it is
That the kings of the earth lay down
Their lives for Your sake,
Setting aside their throne and crown.

Your captivated Lovers, in hope
Of joining You, many a trouble did suffer;
But no remedy could they find,
Their cure being the heartache they suffer.

Won't you please grant the Lovers
To join You – that nourishing bread;
What would lessen from the table
Of Your generosity if those starving are fed?

You cannot join the Beloved
Unless you die, O Niyazi;
In Her Land, it is customary that
The soul is taken as a tax on beauty.

7

Yine dil na'tını söyler Muhammed
Dil ü cân mülkünü toylar Muhammed

Once again my tongue
Gives you praise, O Muhammad!
Heart and Soul host your domain,
O Muhammad!

How can I be capable of praising you,
It is God who gives
The perfect praise to you,
O Muhammad!

As You are the Sultan
Of both worlds,
How can creatures be capable
Of praising You, O Muhammad!

Wearing the robe
Of "If it weren't for you ..."
The cypresses have cast shadows,
O Muhammad!

The Sun and the Moon
Take their light from your face,
Your tresses are the Longest Nights,
O Muhammad!

It's your eyebrows that are
"Two bows' length or even nearer,"
Your skin, the fragrance of roses
O Muhammad!

Stunned by your eyes,
They bowed themselves,
There in the lawn — the hyacinths,
O Muhammad!

Your lips are rubies,
Your mouth, a bed of pearls,
Your tongue speaks of
God's revelation, O Muhammad!

In the time when you ascended to
And roamed the heavens,
There you attained eminence
In the Presence, O Muhammad!

There all the spirits,
All the Prophets, and all the angels
Came to glorify you,
O Muhammad!

Enthroning you
As the King of Knowledge,
They all have become your community,
O Muhammad!

How could they not be your community?
Since, they found in you
The consent of God,
O Muhammad!

Nothing would ever bring you down
From your loftiness
If you interceded for Niyazi,
O Muhammad!

8

Zulmet-i hicrinde bîdâr olmuşam ya Rab meded
İntizâr-ı subh-ı dîdâr olmuşam ya Rab meded

In the darkness of separation from You,
I am sleepless, O Lord, please help!
I am waiting for the morning
Of Your Face, O Lord, please help!

As the East Wind carried the breeze
From the Rose Garden of Union,
I have become the nightingale
Of that Rose Garden, O Lord, please help!

Today, I am left alone and estranged
In the dungeon of the body;
I have been moaning in tears in this cage,
Night and day, O Lord, please help!

Since You served me Wine
On the Day of Alast,
Ever after, I have been drunk
On soberness, O Lord, please help!

Wherever I go, the Fire of Love
Burns me;
Burning and burning, I have become
Only fire, O Lord, please help!

In the Land of Unity, I was Your Lover,
What has befallen me, then?
In multiplicity, I have become the slave
Of the world, O Lord, please help!

This Niyazi has fallen like Joseph
Into the well of existence;
Take hold of my hand and deliver me,
For I am helpless, O Lord, please help!

9

Âriflere esrâr-ı Hüdâ'dan haberim var
Âşıklara dildâr-ı bekâdan haberim var

Of the secrets of God,
To the Gnostics, I have tidings to tell;
Of the Everlasting Beloved,
To the Lovers, I have tidings to tell.

O you whose breast has burnt
With the fire of separation, come,
Of many a remedy for your very sore,
I have tidings to tell.

If you are devoid of life, come,
Pay attention to my words,
Of the Life-bestowing Breath,
I have tidings to tell.

Ahmed said the Face of Adam
Corresponds to the Face of the Beloved;
Of what these words do imply,
I have tidings to tell.

Enter the School of Gnosis
And study the knowledge of Adam;
Of that primal knowledge,
To the scholars, I have tidings to tell.

The seven verses of the Surah of Fatiha
Have been written on his Face;
Of the verses of God in Adam,
I have tidings to tell.

I have found, O Niyazi,
The Divine Attributes in Adam;
Of him where the attributes
Of the Dark Cloud unite, I have tidings to tell.

10

Ey garîb bülbül diyârın kandedir
Bir haber ver gül'izârın kandedir

O forlorn Nightingale, where is your homeland?
Tell me, where is your rosy cheeked Beloved?
You are nobody's lover in this land; yet, surely,
You have a Beloved; tell me, where is She?

Day by day, your lamentations have grown loud,
You have got used to moaning and wailing;
In your Love, from whom do you seek guidance?
Where has gone your patience and modesty?

You have no friend; for whom, then, is your yearning?
You have abandoned ease and taken trouble,
You have been confusing night and day in bewilderment;
Tell me, then, where is your night and day?

What did your eyes see when you beheld the Rose?
And, beholding it, what has befallen you?
Nobody has become intimate with your Secret, not ever,
They have never known where your Rider is.

While once flying in heaven, they brought you down,
They fastened you with the bonds of the four elements.
While once you were Light, they named you Niyazi,
Tell me, where is the esteem you had in eternity?

11

Bugün bir meclise vardım oturmuş pend eder vâiz
Okur açmış kitâbım bu halkı ağlatır vâiz

Today, I attended a sermon meeting,
Having sat down, he was admonishing, the preacher;
Having opened his book, he was reading,
And making people weep, the preacher.

Dividing the people of the world into two,
He puts some into heaven,
And throws the others into hell
By his hand from the pulpit, the preacher.

Breathing out fire from his mouth,
He burns the accursed Satan,
As if he is himself is the torment
Of the seven hells — the preacher.

He has filled hell so full that
There is no room left to stand;
Putting people into it, what a weird service
He provides, the preacher.

It behoves him, indeed, to preach,
As he always complains about people;
The name, in this world, of Niyazi is but
The preacher.

12

Dermân arardım derdime derdim bana dermân imiş
Bürhân arardım ashma ashm bana bürhân imiş

I had been looking for a remedy for my heartache,
I found that my heartache is itself a remedy for me;
I had been looking for evidence for my Gnosis,
I found that my Gnosis is itself evidence for me.

I had been looking hither and yon
That the Face of the Friend I might see;
I had been looking for Him in the without,
I found that the Soul within the soul is He.

I had been imagining that I was separate,
That the Friend and I were apart;
Then I knew that One who sees and hears through me
Has always been that Sweetheart.

By fasting, prayer and pilgrimage,
Think not, O bigot, that all has been done;
Gnosis is that which is needed
To be a Perfect Man.

From whence did you come,
And whither will you go?
He is but a beast who knows not
Whence he came, whither he will go.

You need a Guide to inform you
Of God in the Certainty of Truth;
What those with no Guide know
Is but conjecture, not Truth.

Submit not your Heart to a so-called guide,
Since he leads you into difficulty;
He who has a perfected Guide
Is on a path that is most easy.

See now what a word it is,
Not tortuous, straight it is;
All the world is but a Single Face,
Whoever sees that Face, into rapture goes.

Hear what Niyazi says,
Nothing veils God's Face;
There is nought more evident than Him,
Only to the blind, hidden He lays.

13

Hak ilmine bu âlem bir nüsha imiş ancak
Ol nüshada bu Âdem bir nokta imiş ancak

The world is a copy of the knowledge of God —
No other;
In that copy, Adam is but a Point —
No other.

Within that Point
Hidden are thousands of oceans,
This world is but a drop from that ocean —
No other.

Whoever has found the Breath of Adam,
Adam is he,
Otherwise, the outward form is but a shadow —
No other.

All crave for this delight,
Yet it is what the ignoble can never find,
Amongst men, those who attain it are but a fraction —
No other.

Whoever has found a way to that Breath,
Has attained it, O Niyazi!
They are but the Party of Salvation —
No other.

Mef'ulu mefa'ilun mef'ulu mefa'ilun
The secrets of Adam are only in this Breath —
In no other.

14

Gözlerini n'oldu bî-dâr eyledin
Ah u efgâm sana yâr eyledin

What has befallen you?
Your eyes sleep no more;
Sighing and wailing
Have become your dearest ones,
And, with the Fire of Love,
You have made your Heart
Ever-burning!

Why, O Nightingale,
All you do is but wail?
You have set out
To attain the Rose Garden
— Why?

What has befallen you?
Tears pouring down from your eyes;
For what are you crying?
What is the cause
Of your unending heartache?
Is it because you have seen
The Face of the Rose?

Why, O Nightingale,
All you do is but wail?
You have set out
To attain the Rose Garden
— Why?

If you aspire
To this ephemeral rose garden,
It has no permanence,
It goes by swiftly
Unless you perceive the permanence
In this ephemerality.

Why, O Nightingale,
All you do is but wail?
You have set out
To attain the Rose Garden
— Why?

Not losing your resolve,
You have not tarried even for a moment,
Always in tears, you keep going on your way,
No one knows your state,
You are not understood by others.

Why, O Nightingale,
All you do is but wail?
You have set out
To attain the Rose Garden
— Why?

Tell me what your Heart feels
From this much yearning,
Your pain of separation increases
Day by day;
Please, let Niyazi know:

Why, O Nightingale,
All you do is but wail?
You have set out
To attain the Rose Garden
— Why?

15

Dönmek ister gönlüm cümle sivâdan
Dönelim âşıklar Mevlâ derdiyle

My Heart desires to shun that which is other,
Lovers, let us shun, with heartache for God;
My Heart desires to pass by this ephemeral world,
Lovers, let us pass by, with heartache for God.

The lovesick Lover has nothing to do with the world,
The soul of the man of heartache ever burns
And turns with desire to join the Beloved,
Lovers, let us turn, with heartache for God.

The Moon, the Sun, the stars, the nine spheres
And the angels in rows around the Throne,
They all turn in the arena of Your Love,
Lovers, let us turn, with heartache for God.

Condemn not my state, O bigot,
And never denounce my turning — *dawran*;
There I found healing for my soul,
Lovers, let us turn, with heartache for God.

Craving to enter the arena of Love,
I became Mansur on the gallows of "I am the Truth,"
Niyazi is burning with the fire of ardour,
Lovers, let us burn, with heartache for God.

16

Ey gönül gel Hakk'a giden râh bul
Ehl-i derd olup derûnî âh bul

O Heart, come, the Path to God may you find,
Being a man of heartache, the deep moan may you find,
The Sun and the Moon in the Friend's Land may you find:

If Adam you are, *"Samma wajhullah"* may you find,
Wherever you look, beautiful God may you find.

Of the wealth of the world, proud be not,
With the delight of its posts, content be not,
Considering yourself honorable, base be not:

If Adam you are, *"Samma wajhullah"* may you find,
Wherever you look, beautiful God may you find.

Though it is pleasant to worship God,
As is abstention, obedience and compliance,
And though miracles are pleasant for the men of Retreat:

If Adam you are, *"Samma wajhullah"* may you find,
Wherever you look, beautiful God may you find.

His eyes are ever upon you, but yet,
Having lost Him, you look for His trace,
He has shown Himself in things, being in no place:

If Adam you are, *"Samma wajhullah"* may you find,
Wherever you look, beautiful God may you find.

To the Gnostic, in all things, Names are seen,
In all the Names, the Named is seen,
Through this Niyazi, the Truth is seen:

If Adam you are, *"Samma wajhullah"* may you find,
Wherever you look, beautiful God may you find.

17

Hevâ ise yeter gönül gel Allah'a dönelim gel
Sivâ ise yeter ey dil gel Allah'a dönelim gel

Seeking worldly whim? Enough of it!
O Heart, come, let us return to God;
Seeking that which is other? Enough of it!
O Heart, come, let us return to God.

For how long shall we love the world?
For how long shall we be apart?
Seeking union with the Beloved,
Come, let us return to God.

You crave not the Beloved,
You have been deceived by the world,
The evil-commanding self has led you astray,
Come, let us return to God.

Be awake at the break of dawn,
And moan from deep within,
Only the Lovers have found Him,
Come, let us return to God.

Let us ask those who know,
Those who drink the fragrance of the Rose,
And those who have joined Her,
Come, let us return to God.

Sharing the state of Niyazi,
Be his companion on his Path;
Tears pouring from our eyes,
Come, let us return to God.

18

Padişâhâ aşkım hem-hâne kıl
Masivâ-yı aşkım bî-gâne kıl

O King, my companion let Your Love be;
Indifferent to others than Your Love, let me be.

Let me be pure light
Through my remembrance and meditation of You;
A bewildered drunk and a rapturous Lover,
Let me be.

It is my self that separates me from You;
Tear down the city of my existence,
And laid to waste, let me be.

Cut off the inclination of my spirit to others;
To the candle of Your Beauty, a moth let me be.

Make my Heart a mirror to the Face of Your Essence,
And, with that self-manifestation, a drunk let me be.

Filling my Cup with the Wine of Your intoxicating Effusion,
A tavern, let Niyazi, Your servant, be.

19

Âdetim budur ezelden günde bir şân olurum
Derilip gâh cem olup gâhi perîşân olurum

Since eternity, it has been my custom
To be upon some task each day;
Now, I become gathered together,
And now dispersed I become.

One by one, I call by
Every single thing of this creation;
Gathering all those clothes,
A clothes bazaar I become.

Now cloud, now rain,
Now hail, now snow,
Now plant, now animal,
Now human I become.

Now a Christian, now a Jew,
Now a heathen, now a fire worshipper,
Now a Shiite, now a Sunni Muslim
I become.

Now a worshipper, now an ascetic,
Now an infidel;
Now the knower, now the known,
Now the knowledge, Gnosis,
I become.

Now I become copper and tin,
Now I become gold and silver,
Now a mine for all the minerals
Of the world I become.

Now I become the most degraded
Specimen of a mortal,
Now Solomon who rules
All throughout Qaf I become.

Now my place is narrower than
The narrowest gap;
Now a lofty arena wider than
The Throne and the Footstool I become.

Now I become a grain
On this threshing floor, that is, the world,
Now an arena, vast,
Encompassing all I become.

I become now existent, now nonexistent,
Now existence, now nonexistence I become;
Now through self-manifestation I become manifest,
And now hidden I become.

Now this world, now the hereafter,
Now the Day of Judgement, now the Bridge,
Now the Isthmus, now Heaven,
Now the Fires I become.

Now the Angel of Hell, now the fire,
Now a poisonous oleander, now Hell,
Now a Houri, now a Youth,
Now the Angel of Heaven I become.

Now a speck, now the Sun,
Now the Moon, now the stars,
Now the earth, now the heavens,
Now the Throne of the Merciful I become.

One by one I dressed myself up
In all those myriad garments of forms;
Now stripped of all of them,
All-naked I become.

Though in manifoldness
I am called Mısri,
In the World of Oneness,
The Secret of God I become.

20

Nice bir mekr ü hiyel nekbet-i Deccâl nice bir
Nice bir ey dîni yok mezhebi yok dâl nice bir

For how long will there be deceptions and tricks,
For how long will there be Dajjal's calamities?
O infidel, you who have no religion
And creed – for how long?

For how long will you slay justice
And revive sedition?
I will lay my neck before you,
Strike it and kill me – for how long?

If you made even the religious scholar
Become like you,
His judgement is but sedition
And trick – for how long?

I am ready! If you are skilled,
Come, let us meet!
Shoot the arrow or swing the mace
Of your knowledge – for how long?

Can Dajjal's evil be warded off by words?
O Mısri, if you have attained a state,
That's enough for you;
Words – for how long?

21

Ey kudret ıssı pâdişâh lûtfeyle açıver yolum
Bağlandı her yanım ey şâh lûtfeyle açıver yolum

O King of Omnipotence,
Grace me with opening my way;
I am fettered, O King,
Grace me with opening my way.

By Your Essential Name,
By all Your Attributes,
By Your glory and subsistence,
Grace me with opening my way.

By the Supreme Name,
By the Generous Light,
By the Praise of the Universe,
Grace me with opening my way.

You made me human out of Your grace,
You made me happy with Your presence,
You made me sad with Your absence,
Grace me with opening my way.

You had me chase a quarry
To let me, capturing it, find You;
Alas, the base world fettered me,
Grace me with opening my way.

My evil self has led me astray
And has obstructed all the roads;
O Graceful, from You is the help,
Grace me with opening my way.

This soul seeks Union again,
Seeks oneness with You, O Sultan,
The Heart seeks help to attain You,
Grace me with opening my way.

Whenever we see a Perfect Man,
Beholding him, we feel remorseful of ourselves;
Thus, we return to You and beseech:
Grace me with opening my way.

O Lord, helpless are Your servants
To find the right way to You;
You are the remedy for all the heartaches,
Grace me with opening my way.

Make Remembrance the companion
Of my tongue, till it reaches the heart
And leads the way from land to land,
Grace me with opening my way.

Niyazi, the Lover with heartache, is helpless,
He is fettered by the four elements;
O God, the world is but a deceptive lure,
Grace me with opening my way.

22

Essalâ her kim gelir bâzâr-ı aşka essalâ
Essalâ her kim yanarsa nâr-ı aşka essalâ

As-sala! to him who comes
To the Bazaar of Love, *as-sala!*
As-sala! to him who burns
With the Fire of Love, *as-sala!*

As-sala! to him who becomes Mansur today
On the gallows of "I am the Truth,"
To him who, giving up his soul,
Is hanged for the sake of Love, *as-sala!*

To him who abandons
His crown and throne like Ibn Adham,
To that Naked Abdal,
To that Sultan of Love, *as-sala*!

Like Abraham, the Lover casts
Himself into fires — to that Nightingale
Of the Rose Garden of Love,
Wholeheartedly, *as-sala*!

Laying waste the mountain of existence,
He renders it a road to the Beloved's Land;
O Niyazi, to that Architect of Love,
Say, *as-sala*!

23

Ol menem kim vâkıf-ı esrâr-ı ilm-i Âdem'im
Kâşif-i genc-i hakîkat hem hayât-ı âlemim

I am cognizant of the secrets
Of the knowledge Adam has;
It is me who opens the treasure of reality,
It is me who is the life of the Universe.

The secrets of the Unseen
Are hidden in me;
I hold the secret of the Trust,
That Treasure Unknown is within me.

I have seen the Beauty of God
To be manifest in every single thing;
It thus makes me joyful to behold those mirrors,
That is, every manifest thing.

All my words have been a key
To open the Hidden Treasure;
In my every breath,
With the Breath of Jesus, I am familiar.

To the Single Being
I have given all that there is;
Now, I never breathe, not even an instant,
Without Your Essence, Names and Attributes.

On me is reliant
All that is on earth and in heaven;
I am the Supreme Talisman,
Be it manifest or hidden.

I am Mısri, I have become the king
Of the land of my being;
Though engendered,
The Primordial Secret am I
In the meaning.

24

Elâ ey mürşid-i âlem haber ver ilm-i Mevlâ'dan
Elâ ey ma'nâ-yı Âdem haber ver remz-i esmâdan

Now, O Guide of the whole world,
Tell me of the knowledge of God.
Now, O meaning of Adam,
Tell me of the signification of the Names.

What secret is Adam and Eve?
What secret is "He taught all the Names"?
What secret is Sidra and Tooba?
Tell me of the High Throne.

What is the twofold knowledge on tongues?
What is the symbol of Zulkarnain?
What place is where two seas meet?
Tell me of Khidr and Moses.

What place is the Lowest Center?
What place is the Middle Circle?
Unknown is the Great Point,
Tell me of the Small one.

Who effuses spirit and makes the dead revive?
And what secret is the Breath of Jesus?
What is the ocean in Mary?
Tell me of the Peerless Pearl.

What are the secrets of the Koran?
What are the lights of the secrets?
What is the conduct of Mahdi?
Tell me of the secret of the Night Journey.

What is Mısri? What is Canaan?
Who is Flawless? And who is the Instant?
The Koran told me of this,
Tell me of the Seven Reciters.

25

Câmm terk etmeden cânâm arzularsın
Zünnârım kesmeden imâm arzularsın

Without abandoning your soul,
For the Sweetheart you aspire;
Without cutting away your Belt
Still for Faith you aspire.

Like yonder children,
You ride on a stick horse;
Without a polo-stick and ball,
Still for the arena you aspire.

While you are plodding,
Little by little, like an ant;
Still for the journey
Far beyond the angels you aspire.

You surmise the ankle-deep puddle
To be the sea;
Without abandoning the drop,
Still for the Ocean you aspire.

O Niyazi, come,
Shoot not your arrow far;
Without being a servant with heartache,
Still for the Sultan you aspire.

26

Serây-ı din esâsıdır şeri'at
Tarîk-i Hak hüdâsıdır şeri'at

The ground of the palace of religion is Divine Law,
The guidance to the Path of God is Divine Law.

It is the first gate to the Presence of God,
The beginning of the Path is Divine Law.

And through it, these roads come to an end,
The very end of the Path is Divine Law.

The call of the Heralds, calling people
To the Straight Path, is Divine Law.

It is the deeds of the Prophets;
The guidance for all is Divine Law.

On the Night of Ascent, God's bestowal
Upon His Most Beloved is Divine Law.

For twenty three years, from Gabriel to him,
The revelation of God is Divine Law.

There is many a kind of knowledge in the world,
The ultimate one is Divine Law.

To kill the unbeliever, that is, the self,
The predestined ordinance of God is Divine Law.

The Men of Heart wage the Great War;
The joy of their Hearts is Divine Law.

In the front of the Caravan of the Path,
The leader and guide is Divine Law.

Although Reality is sultanhood,
Its banner in the front is Divine Law.

The Friend of God is never a stranger to it,
With what he is intimate is Divine Law.

On It subsist heavens and earth,
The frame of this building is Divine Law.

Men of deviation can never know the Holy Law;
The enemy of those enemies is Divine Law.

And in their narrow minds, they surmise that
For the establishment of order is Divine Law.

Take heed, O friend, follow them not,
Never set at naught Divine Law.

Without Divine Law, Reality turns into deviation;
Reality is Light, its radiance is Divine Law.

Were there no radiance, there would be no Light,
To Reality comparable is Divine Law.

No Friend of God comes to the world
Without a staff in his hand, that is, Divine Law.

And It is his cap and shawl and garment,
Also, on his back, his cloak is Divine Law.

Reality is but the soul of the Friend of God,
And that which is beyond his soul is Divine Law.

When the soul is taken away, the body dies;
When the secret is taken away, there remains Divine Law.

Without the soul the body cannot subsist;
That on which Reality subsists is Divine Law.

Reality is like a beautiful women,
And Her golden garment is Divine Law.

Do not undress Her before strangers,
Her bashful side is Divine Law.

Reality is the High Throne, without doubt,
Whose covering is but Divine Law.

For all the Prophets and the Friends of God,
O Niyazi, the guide is Divine Law.

27

Nevbahâr erişti bîdâr olayım şimden geru
Andelîb-i bâğ-ı gülzâr olayım şimden geru

Here comes the spring,
I shall be sleepless from now on;
I shall be the Nightingale
Of the Rose Garden from now on.

Like an Abdal, leaving behind passion
For this world and for the hereafter,
I shall open the casket
Of secrets from now on.

Beating the drum of "I am the Truth,"
Like Mansur,
I shall enter the place of execution
And be hanged from now on.

Abandoning all that there is,
Like Ibrahim Adham, I shall be a wanderer
Through all countries and lands
From now on.

For how long shall I abide
In this lowland of the body?
I shall ascend to heavens
And be revolving from now on.

Devastating these lands
Of relativities and bounds,
I shall be journeying in the Land
Of No-Place from now on.

I shall make the bird-soul happy,
Letting it fly from this cage;
I shall fly to the city of non-existence
From now on.

Now, there remains only this body
Belonging to me;
Obliterating it, too, I shall become
Existent from now on.

Let there remain not
Even a speck of Mısri's being;
I shall be set free and join the Beloved
From now on.

28

Oldum çü mahv-ı mahz-ı zât buldum vücûdumdan necât
Ben içmişem âb-ı hayat irmez bana hergiz memât

Being annihilated in Sheer Essence,
I have been delivered from my being, for ever;
Having drunk the Water of Life,
Death cannot reach me, not ever.

I have abandoned all I had
For the sake of the Friend;
Leaving behind both denial and faith,
I've become steady in the All-Evident.

Whatsoever I behold,
To mine eyes the Secret of Eternity appears;
When everything attains God,
Into nothingness the world vanishes.

Since I have been a friend of the Friend,
Since I have drunk His Wine with pleasure,
Most hospitably has He been treating my soul,
What I enjoy is but sweet and sugar.

Coming out of Retreat,
I have found Oneness in multiplicity;
Having put the Retreat up for sale in the bazaar,
My night is acquittal and my day, festivity.

I have seen that all these worlds
Are contained in my being;
Heaven and Hell have been unified,
All has become my attributes — everything.

To whichever direction I incline,
Everything inclines to that direction;
O Niyazi, all your shadows
Have been the six directions.

29

Uyan gözün aç durma yalvar güzel Allah'a
Yolundan izin ayırma yalvar güzel Allah'a

Wake up, open your eyes, stand not still,
Beseech Beautiful God.
Go not astray from His Path,
Beseech Beautiful God.

Every night keep a vigil of prayer,
Every day be at fasting,
Ever invoke His Name,
Beseech Beautiful God.

Some day these eyes will not see,
Some day these ears will not hear;
Before this chance is lost,
Beseech Beautiful God.

Know that health is a gift,
And each hour, a provision,
Worship in secrecy,
Beseech Beautiful God.

Waste not your life for nothing,
Cast not yourself into fire;
Lie not asleep day and night,
Beseech Beautiful God.

For how long will you sleep, arise,
Keep not yourself aloof from this joy;
His ocean of generosity is abundant,
Beseech Beautiful God.

At every break of dawn
A thousand favours come down from God;
At that time, your Heart awakens,
Beseech Beautiful God.

Invoking the Name of God,
Make the soul and the Heart joyful;
Sing like the nightingale,
Beseech Beautiful God.

Now, come, with Niyazi,
Supplicate to God;
Keep your prayer requests long,
Beseech Beautiful God.

30

Sırr-ı Hakk'ı nicesi fâş eyleyem ben ey sikât
K'am ancak remz ile etmiş beyân ehl-i nikât

How, O Trusted Ones,
Could I reveal the secret of God?
Since men of subtle meanings
Only by allusions have spoken of it.

The more I unconceal Him,
The more He is concealed;
Whereas He is evident by Himself,
Proofs and demonstrations do veil Him.

He who enjoys the Oneness of the Truth
Unifies Him not, unlike the man of association;
For his tongue has become speechless
And his intellect has been checkmated.

That which is highest of the high
Is also present beneath the earth;
His Essence is One, but many a thousand
Attributes were made manifest.

Though He is One in His Essence,
Endless are His Attributes,
See this lamp-glass whose candle
Is the Light of the Essence.

All is, manifest or unmanifest,
Naught but a lantern;
Its glass is the contingent beings,
And its candle, Man.

O Niyazi, as Adam has become
The lustre of the world,
From his breath the Spirit of Life
Is bestowed upon all the world.

31

Çıkıp hüccâc ile gitmek ne güzeldir ne güzeldir
Yolunda câm terk etmek ne güzeldir ne güzeldir

Going on pilgrimage with pilgrims,
How pleasant, how pleasant!
Abandoning the self for Your sake,
How pleasant, how pleasant!

The sufferings on the way to the Kaaba
Melt away all the sins;
The pilgrimage and the delights of joining,
How pleasant, how pleasant!

The thorns on the way to the Kaaba
Are but a rose garden for the Lovers,
The road to and the caravan of Hejaz,
How pleasant, how pleasant!

Reaching the city of Madina,
Seeing the tomb of the Most Beloved,
Laying the face upon its threshold,
How pleasant, how pleasant!

Traversing the mountain passes,
Would that the journey be accomplished,
Would that the lands of the Kaaba be seen,
How pleasant, how pleasant!

It is the place of sight for the Prophets,
It is the dwelling place of the Friends of God;
Seeing it, the Kaaba of God,
How pleasant, how pleasant!

Would that it be the portion of Niyazi
To reach there and to find what he seeks;
Would that he be full of joy and delight,
How pleasant, how pleasant!

32

Zuhûr-u kâinatın mâdenisin ya Resulallah
Rumûz-u "küntü kenz"in mahzenisin ya Resulallah

You are the mine
Of the manifestation of the universe,
O Messenger of God!
You are the repository of the Hidden Treasure,
O Messenger of God!

In this world, in outward form and person
You are called human;
In your Essential Reality, you are not,
O Messenger of God!

Your being gathers together
The whole existence,
And your knowledge encompasses all,
O Messenger of God!

From your mouth
The secrets of God-given knowledges spring,
You are intimate with the Knowledge of Realities,
O Messenger of God!

You are the Commander of all
Who came to this world,
And also who will come,
O Messenger of God!

In the garden of the universe, Man is a tree,
And the leaves are all the rest;
The Prophets are the fruits,
And you are the quintessence of them,
O Messenger of God!

If you did not intercede for Niyazi,
Existence would annihilate him;
You are the salve
For the wound of his being,
O Messenger of God!

33

Hatm-i cem'il-mürselînin fahridir fakr u fenâ
Hatm odur kim bir ola yamnda hem şâh u gedâ

Poverty and Nothingness is the glory
Of the Seal of all the Messengers;
The Seal he is, in the presence of whom
All become one, kings and beggars.

Worldly prominence makes you
In need of status;
Prominence it is that makes you
Rich beyond that very need of status.

Know that following the instructions
Of the intellect a proof cannot be;
Follow the instructions of God
That a guide may your knowledge be.

If even Moses wants to be his disciple,
Khidr does not accept him;
Since he must never ask "how?" and "why?",
The one who accompanies him.

If it is glory you seek,
Await the door of humility, there leave not;
Keep yourself boiling on violent fires,
Till the golden elixir comes out.

"Two bows' length or even nearer"
— Abide not there, in that station;
Burning with the Lights of the Sheer Essence,
Attain the Last Station.

For Mısri, the Ultimate Station
Has been the abandonment of everything;
Neither within nor without,
Save God, there remained nothing.

34

Ey şeh bu zen-i dünyamn gel ahna aldanma
Şem'-i ruh nârına pervâne gibi yanma

O friend! Come, be not seduced
By the beauty of that perfidious woman,
That is, the world.
Her rosy cheek is a candle, burning;
Like a moth, with its fire, burn not.
Her beauty is ephemeral,
With its lustre yourself tarnish not.
Be not bewitched by her vows and promises,
Them believe not.

True are my words, them do not deny,
Submit yourself to the truths,
Think not every word is a lie.

The world is a seven-headed,
A thousand-toothed dragon
With a thousand mouths in each head,
In which each morsel is another son of Adam.
Its poison is antidote,
And its antidote is poison,
If you drink its sweet drink,
It is not sweet drink — it is blood.

True are my words, them do not deny,
Submit yourself to the truths,
Think not every word is a lie.

Many a king has been checkmated
By this world,
None of them was ever satisfied
With its dignity and wealth;
Take lesson from its month and year,
See how quickly each of them
Comes to an end.

True are my words, them do not deny,
Submit yourself to the truths,
Think not every word is a lie.

Intellect can never be aware
Of any of its delusions,
This knowledge of yours fails
To recognize its disguised Satan;
However much you revile it, it never minds
And it deludes you with sweet words,
Easily got rid of, it is not.

True are my words, them do not deny,
Submit yourself to the truths,
Think not every word is a lie.

O Mısri, these words are for you,
Try to take lesson from them;
Making poverty the praise,
Never grovel before the world,
And, having been healed of
The very illness of ignorance,
Never bear a grudge against anyone.

True are my words, them do not deny,
Submit yourself to the truths,
Think not every word is a lie.

35

Vallahi Deccâl senin emeklerin hebâdur
Çalıştığın sihirler ha bir kuru anâdur

I swear, O Dajjal,
To waste all your efforts do go.
The sorceries that you practice
Are all but vain trouble and ado.

God encompasses you,
All your tasks creates He;
Be wary of the Divine Deception,
Nuisance it is, the honey you fancy.

Watch out; your tricks of sorcery
Are going to return to you;
So, dig not the pit
Deeper than the length of you.

Also watch out whether your enemy
Has prepared a deception for you;
Be wary of the forsaken one,
One who is under God's protection.

The silkworm eats leaves, laughing,
While the mulberry cries;
But whereas the mulberry recovers its leaves,
At his end the worm dies.

However numerous
The silkworm army may be,
Entering into cocoons, those soldiers
Are nourishment for the mulberry.

Do not tread him beneath your feet
When you see Mısri in the mud;
If you are cruel against the downtrodden,
Against you, so is God.

36

Ben sanırdım âlem içre bana hiç yâr kalmadı
Ben beni terk eyledim gördüm ki agyâr kalmadı

I had been thinking that, for me,
Within the world, no beloved there remained;
But, when I abandoned myself, I saw that
Other than the Beloved none remained — anymore.

In all things I had been seeing but the thorn
Without there being any rose;
Now, all the world has become a Rose Garden,
No thorn remained — anymore.

I had been weeping and wailing in my Heart;
Then, I know not what has befallen me,
They have all ceased,
No sighs, no tears remained — anymore.

Manifoldness vanished with the appearance of Oneness,
Now, I am in seclusion with the Friend;
The whole universe has become the Truth,
No shops or bazaars there remained — anymore.

Religion and piety, habits and pride,
Have all gone with the wind;
O Niyazi, what has befallen you? With you,
No restraint of piousness remained — anymore.

37

Cümle eşyâya birer hâlet konulmuştur tamâm
Birbirinden ba'zı nâkıs ba'zın istidâdı tam

All things have been set in a manner:
Some are more deficient,
And some are more perfect than another.
In a word, what is the formation
Which is perfect in nature?
Love it is, Love is that perfect formation,
Wine's concealment of heat
And the reed-flute's impressing sound
All come from It.

Since the Rose Garden of Oneness
Is the Heart in Love,
The delight of Union comes through Love;
And he who abandons both worlds
Is ever intoxicated by Love.
The vale of bewilderment is indeed
The Station of Love, there being
In that vale the beggar
Not distinguished from the king.

Divine Love
Is the best companion of the Gnostic;
Drinking the Wine of the Essence,
His every breath becomes the Spirit, Life-bestowing.
And, seeing the places of manifestation
As the very Self of the Manifest,
He suffers no more grief — it is over.
In the retired chamber of the secret of Oneness,
The Lover and the Beloved,
Are never parted from one another.

If you want to be among the People of Truth,
Abandon your sanctimonious worship;
And have your inside purified, giving up pretension.
Pay heed to admonitions with insight,
Abandon yourself from dissipation.
Ask not the Lovers to abandon
Drawing upon themselves the blame;
Tell me, is it possible to change
God's pre-determination?

For the Truthful One, the pillar of life
Is but abandoning himself from his being;
His Heart should ever burn
With every strike of lightning —
A Lover is he over whom thunderbolts cease not.
The Pen of Love crossed out the letter,
That is, the Lover's being,
That, through the negation of that which is other,
He would be established
In confirming God's Being.

O Niyazi, in Love
You have found delight without a beginning,
And through the confirmation of the Beloved,
You have found delight free of "La"
— A delight, perpetual and everlasting.
O Fuzuli, in Love
You have found unending delight;
Such is every task, if you start with
"In the Name of God".

Note on the poem:
This poem was written in the poetical form called *tahmis*. It is a form in which a poet
writes a poem, adding extra lines to another poet's poem. Below, the italic lines refer
to the original lines of the poem by Fuzuli, and others are the extra lines added by
Niyazi Mısri.

38

Zât-ı Hak'da mahrem-i irfân olan anlar bizi
İlm-i sırda bahr-ı bî-pâyân olan anlar bizi

Being immersed in the Essence of God,
He who is familiar with Gnosis
Understands us;
Arriving at the knowledge of the Secret,
He who has become the Shoreless Ocean,
Understands us.

Those seeking the ephemeral rose garden
Understand not;
But he who is stunned by the Beauty
Of the Everlasting Face
Understands us.

We have left behind straightening up
This world and the hereafter;
Collapsing totally,
He who has become ruined
Understands us.

We are the Abdals, we who have removed
Our shawls from our shoulders;
Stripping off his being,
He who has become Naked
Understands us.

He who knows not trial and grace
To be the same, suffers torment;
Delivering himself from that torment,
He who has become a Sultan
Understands us.

O bigot, walking in sobriety,
In no way you can understand us;
Sipping a draught of Pure Wine,
He who has gotten drunk
Understands us.

One has to be a Man
To conceive the words of the Gnostic;
Think not that, in this world,
He who is a beast
Understands us.

O Niyazi, today we have let our drop
Merge into the Ocean;
The drop understands not,
It is but the Ocean that
Understands us.

Having abandoned the world,
We have been traversing
The Land of No-Place, O Mısri!
Since then,
He who is the Sweetheart of the souls
Understands us.

39

Uyan gafletten ey gâfil seni aldatmasın dünyâ
Yakam al elinden kim seni sonra kılar rüsvâ

O heedless one, from heedlessness, awake!
Let not this world deceive you.
Shake it off! Or else, a disgrace of you it will make.

Of this perfidious one what do you imagine?
You loved it so much, and one who loves it
Lays aside his religion.

Be not at enmity with anyone! For you,
Your very self is enough to be an enemy,
Which, to the last, never leaves you.

You have heard from God's Messenger
Many a verse and message; but, alas,
You take not benefit from them, not ever.

Turn your Soul and Heart to me, veiling
Your outward eyes, so that you may sense
Within each word jewel-like meaning.

Of the words of Mustafa, enjoy the delight,
Even a thousand "manna and quails"
Cannot match that delight.

For true wealth, read the verses of the Koran
That, within each letter, O Niyazi,
A thousand peerless pearls you may find.

40

Bahr içinde katreyim bahr oldu hayrân bana
Ferş içinde zerreyim arş oldu seyrân bana

Though I am just a drop in it,
The Ocean marvels at me;
Though I am just a speck on the earth,
Throughout the whole universe I journey.

Having seen the Friend evidently,
Nothing hidden there remained for me;
If the world were to drown in the Flood,
That Flood would only be a drop to me.

What have I to do with outward form?
My mine is within me;
If Doomsday came today,
No suffering would touch me.

I am Anqa dwelling in Qaf, that is, the Heart,
I am familiar with the Secret of Reality;
The sultan of thoughts am I,
"Man" is just the name of me.

It is Yunus speaking
Through the tongue of Niyazi;
As everyone is in need of a soul,
Yunus is the soul for me.

41

Hak yolunun rehberi nefesidir kâmilin
Dil tahtının serveri nefesidir kâmilin

The Guide to the Path of God
Is the Breath of the Perfect Man;
What is most prominent in the Heart
Is the Breath of the Perfect Man.

That which overcomes your self,
That which wards off death,
That which breathes out Life
Is the Breath of the Perfect Man.

Go seek Adam
And find Adam in Adam;
The secret of "He has breathed out"
Is the Breath of the Perfect Man.

Reading the Surah of The Star,
Conceive what God's revelation is;
Know that that Word of God
Is the Breath of the Perfect Man.

The Breath of the Holy Spirit
— Ask for it from Adam;
That which enlivens the Heart
Is the Breath of the Perfect Man.

That which is called the kernel of Essence,
That which is called the effusion of salvation,
That which is called the Water of Life
Is the Breath of the Perfect Man.

That which enlivens the bodies,
That which exhilarates the souls,
That which revives the dead
Is the Breath of the Perfect Man.

If he blows a breath onto the dead,
A voice is heard from all directions;
One that resurrects all, O friend,
Is the Breath of the Perfect Man.

That which enlivens Niyazi,
That which makes him, the speck, a spring,
That which makes him, the drop, an ocean
Is the Breath of the Perfect Man.

42

Şunlar ki görüp yüzünü bu dâra gelirler
Ol ahde vefâ eyleyip ikrâra gelirler

After having seen Your Face,
Those who come to this abode
Remained faithful to their covenant with You,
Here, to profess, they come.

Those whose eyes have been fixed
On Your Hair from eternity,
Know You not,
And here, to deny, they come.

The Abdals of Divinity,
Having drunk from the Cup of Your Eye,
To whirl with that Love,
To this world, they come.

Those whose Hearts have been
Twined round Your Hair;
Entering into the place of execution,
Like Mansur, upon the gallows, they come.

See the seeds growing up,
Firstly, into trees;
From them, with their secret within,
Once again, the fruits come.

When you collect the seeds
Of trees of any kind and plant them;
They, again, give the fruits
Of the trees from which they come.

None of them ever stray
From Your way;
Treading their own peculiar path,
To the bazaar, they come.

What if their paths are diverse?
All of them are Your Lovers,
They all seek You,
And, to You, O Beloved, they come.

For sure, those who enter
Into this garden, O Niyazi,
First roam through thorns,
And, at last, to the Rose Garden, they come.

43

Bu halvete bakma güzâf zevk u safâ halvettedir
Halvetle kıl içini sâf nûr u ziyâ halvettedir

Deem not this Retreat as vain,
Enjoyment and delight is in Retreat;
With Retreat have your inside purified,
Light and illumination is in Retreat.

It makes you know your self,
It makes you die before you die,
It makes you sense the Path of Annihilation,
Poverty and annihilation is in Retreat.

He becomes a restless ocean,
Turbulent with its immersing waves;
He loses himself in rapture,
The Love of God is in Retreat.

Having fallen into fires,
The Stars, the Sun and the Moon burn;
Earth stands still, and heavens revolve,
Earth and heavens are in Retreat.

Be wide awake, behold attentively,
All is One, be it near or be it far;
Tongue and lips become silent,
Union with God is in Retreat.

O you who seek union in separation,
O you who seek comfort in trouble,
O you who seek the joy of drinking in Oneness,
Drinking and Subsistence are in Retreat.

Abandon yourself, O Niyazi,
Come, unify the soul and the body;
If you want to sense the Secret,
The Secret of God is in Retreat.

44

Tâ ezelden biz bu aşk içinde rüsvâ olmuşuz
İsmimizdir söylenen mânada Anka olmuşuz

From the beginning of eternity,
We have been ravaged by Love;
It is our name which is spoken,
In meaning, Anqa we have become.

They surmised that we were in multiplicity
In the world of myriad forms;
Yet, within multiplicity,
Single and alone we have become.

What if we put on those garments
Of relativities and individuation;
Stripping them off,
Spiritually Naked we have become.

We speak with the obscure lexicon
Of the Speech of Birds;
Not everyone understands us,
Since riddles we have become.

How could they understand us
Through words and form and body?
We are neither words nor form,
Pure meaning we have become.

Drops met the river,
And, the river met the Ocean;
All have gathered, joining one another,
That Ocean, we have become.

Sparks met the Sun,
The Sun met the source of Oneness;
There remained no multiplicity,
Single and one, we have become.

Multiplicity shows relativity
In the mirror;
Wiping out that dust of worry,
Polished, we have become.

What the bigot invokes
Is the outward form — the letter and voice;
The invoker and the Invoked
And the invocation, we have become.

We do not vociferously invoke Him
Like the sufis;
Joining the Ocean, insulated
From that voice, we have become.

Come, if you are a locus of manifestation
Of "He taught all the Names";
Both Adam and the Names
Taught to him, we have become.

Seek not to see Mısri through outward form
And with your outer eyes;
For, within the Qaf of outward form,
Anqa, we have become.

45

Mevâlîdin sana her fasl u bâb
Kitâbün fî kitâbün fî kitab

For you, each portion
Of the three kingdoms of nature
Is a book within a book
Within a book.

Through your attainment of them,
In each of those books, there is
An answer within an answer
Within an answer.

Also, in the both worlds
And in the isthmus,
There is a veil within a veil
Within a veil.

Knowledges and form,
And the meaning-Reality
Is wine within wine
Within wine.

From those three,
My Secret receives
An addressing within addressing
Within addressing.

For one who abandons
Saying "you," "I" and "he,"
There is no reckoning within reckoning
Within reckoning.

Your ignorance of yourself,
Of your names, and of your attributes, O friend,
Is a blessing within blessing
Within blessing.

Whereas your awareness
Of yourself, of your names, and of your attributes
Is a torment within torment
Within torment.

That which is seen from them
Is the existence of creation
Which is a mirage within mirage
Within mirage.

O Niyazi, the body, the Heart
And the Spirit are said
To be an aspect within aspect
Within aspect.

46

Yine firkat nârına yandı cihân
Hasretâ gitti mübarek Ramazan

Once more the world has been burnt by separation,
O yearning! Gone, the blessed Ramadan!
With Light, the world had found a new soul,
O separation! Gone, the blessed Ramadan!

In it descended the Koran, whose light is beautiful,
Within its Night of Power, whose power is beautiful,
Gone, with beautiful chantings of Unification,
Farewell! Gone, the blessed Ramadan!

Now with glorification and praise and invocation,
Now with gratitude and prayer and thanksgiving,
The dead Hearts were enlivened by Light,
O longing! Gone, the blessed Ramadan!

In this month are fettered, said the Messenger,
The jinns and Satan, lest they make transgression;
All prayers were being accepted,
O separation! Gone, the blessed Ramadan!

Gathering together, let us pray and beseech God,
Let us go straight with the light of the Koran,
Woe unto us, O Niyazi, we did not know its merit,
Alas! Gone, the blessed Ramadan!

47

İnile ey derdli gönül inile ehl-i derdin inleyecek çağıdır
Gel tımâr et yâreni sen aşk ile yârelerin onulacak çağıdır

Moan, O aching Heart, moan,
Now is the time of moaning, for Men of heartache;
Come, heal your wounds with Love,
Now is the time of healing, for the wounds.

I wonder whether he who never makes merry,
Laying in heedlessness, has a soul in his body;
Here they are, the Roses of Oneness, they all bloomed,
Now is the time of lamentation, for the nightingale.

In eternity, you were intimate with the King,
For trial, you have been sent to this land;
It behoves you now to lament your affliction,
Now is the time of shedding tears, for the eyes.

My Heart has no patience, I don't know why,
It resolves to tear my body apart;
It wants to go to the Owner from this wilderness,
Now is the time of resolving to attain the Origin.

O Niyazi, he who is not a man of pride
Is ever at ease in this world;
Conceive God before you pass away,
Now is the time of arrival of the Messenger of Death.

48

Ey kerîm Allah ey ganî Sultân
Derdliyiz senden umanz dermân

O You Generous God, O You Rich Sultan,
We are heart aching Lovers, from You we seek the remedy.
You have endless grace, Your benevolence is boundless,
We are heart aching Lovers, from You we seek the remedy.

Though your servants have many a sin,
Your Mercy exceeds their wrongdoings;
None grants us succour but You,
We are heart aching Lovers, from You we seek the remedy.

If You did not bid us, the sinners, to come unto You,
No man would be able to reach You;
We are incurable if You do not grant us the cure,
We are heart aching Lovers, from You we seek the remedy.

You have bestowed a gift,
A gift, from Your Most Holy Effusion, which brings
Thousands of joys, for the place of each suffering,
We are heart aching Lovers, from You we seek the remedy.

This Niyazi seeks to invoke You,
His heart, night and day, seeks to contemplate You;
Whoever attains to Your Essence, gives thanks to You,
We are heart aching Lovers, from You we seek the remedy.

49

İster isen marifette olasın âli-cenâb
Ehl-i irfân eşiğinde yüzünü eyle türâb

If you want to be noble
With Gnosis,
Lay your face upon the threshold
Of the Men of Gnosis.

Do not merge yourself with the world,
For awhile, on it set a seal;
You cannot turn it, my friend,
Most heavy is this mill wheel.

To render this place of ruins prosperous
Many a people tried;
While they had one side on the mend,
Fell into ruins, the other side.

People of heedlessness chased too much
After this mirage, imagining it to be water;
None of them could ever find in this desert
Even a drop of water.

For awhile, do not indulge in
The worldly people, keep yourself in isolation;
Veiling your face, on a point
Gather your mind in contemplation.

For awhile, keep the doors
Of your eyes, ears and tongue fastened shut,
Perchance a door to God will be opened
From your Heart.

If you want to deliver yourself
From death, fall in Love;
Burn your body and soul away,
Turning around the Fire of Love.

Step into this tavern of heartache,
From your hand, the cup remove not;
For the Lover there is no Wine
Other than the blood of his Heart.

May this ever be your aspiration,
So that you may comprehend God;
In both worlds, nought is there
More meritorious than knowing God.

If you want to deliver yourself
From Hell's torments,
Attain Gnosis, since from the fire
Of ignorance come all torments.

These are not the words
Of Niyazi, O son, listen;
Hear them from the Four Books
Descended from Heaven.

50

Yakıp aşk odına câm meşâmın bûy'u tevhîd et
Kamuya yek nazar birle şuhûdun rûy'u tevhîd et

Casting yourself upon the Fire of Love,
Everything you sense through it, unify.
With a single look at all-there-is,
Everything you witness, unify.

Be not like the fish; never think yourself
To be far from the Ocean;
It encompasses all:
Look around, unify every direction.

Descend not into the well of imitation,
Ascend to the throne of realization;
Journey from you to you,
Unify yourself through your perception.

Lifting relativities from your sight,
Let your insight be opened, the Truth to see;
And, on beholding Her, unify the Vision
Of the Beloved's beauty.

For the Men of Nearness,
"Samma wajhullah" is the direction of prayer;
O Niyazi, unify the prostration
Upon the Eyebrows, for ever.

GLOSSARY OF TERMS

Abdal	Literally, *Abdal* means 'the exchanged one', that is, one who has changed his human attributes with the divine ones. *Abdal*s are a high-ranked group from among the friends of God.
Abstention	Abstention (*riyada*) is the practice of refraining from the world in order to loosen the power of the self which hinders one from perceiving the reality as it is.
Acquittal	The 15th night of the Month Shabaan is a very blessed night which is called the Night of Acquittal (*Shab-i Baraat*).
Ahmed	It is a name of the Prophet Muhammad, indicating his presence in the station of *Ahadiyya*, the last of the stations.
Alast	This term which is used in the phrases of 'the Day of *Alast*' or 'the Gathering of *Alast*' is derived from the Koran: "'Am I not your Lord?' They said: 'Yes, we testify'" [7:172]. '*Alast*', the Arabic word, used in the beginning of the verse, meaning 'Am I not', is used as an indication of the covenant made between God and the souls of all mankind before they were created as individual beings.

Annihilation	Annihilation of the servant's illusory existence through the obliteration of human attributes and empty whims. And after Annihilation (*Fana*) comes Subsistence (*Baqa*) which is adornmentation of the one who attained Annihilation with the Attributes of God. [See also *Subsistence*]
Anqa	*Anqa*, the unseen Bird, dwells on Mount *Qaf*. *Anqa*, being unseen, symbolizes the meaning behind the apparent form — Mount *Qaf*. In this respect, the body is Mount *Qaf*, and the pure spirit, *Anqa*. There is also another symbolism in which *Qaf* stands for the Heart, and *Anqa*, for the Perfect Man.
As-sala!	'*As-Sala!*' means the exclamation 'Look!' It is also the salawat uttered to call people to Friday prayer or funeral prayer.
Ball	[See *Polo stick*]
Bazaar of Love	The Bazaar of Love is the gathering of the friends of God where the Lover, giving his soul, gets the Beloved in turn.
Beauty	The Beauty (*Jamal*) of God. On the other hand, its opposite, Majesty (*Jalal*) denotes that which is other than God, that is, the world, behind which God veils Himself. Troubles and trials come from the Majesty of God, whereas compassion and provisions come from His Beauty. Being created as a copy of the Divine image, the reality of Adam mirrors Divine Beauty. And his bodily form, being a veil to this mirroring, is the place of manifestation of Majesty.
Belt	The belt symbolizes association of partners with God.
Bewilderment	Shaykh al-Kashani says: "The ocean of Bewilderment (*Hayrah*) is the Unity pervading all and manifesting itself in multiple forms. It is bewildering because the Unity appears in a concrete determined form in every single thing and yet remains non-determined in the whole. It is bewildering because it is non-limitation and limitation."

Bigot	Literally, bigot (*zahid*) means ascetic. The word derives from the term *zuhd*, that is, withdrawal from the worldly things which is itself a sufi practice. However, in poetry it takes a different connotation which enables us to translate it as 'bigot'. The *zahid* or bigot is one who does not engage in worldly things imagining that he has devoted himself to religion. They are known as people who, having not found the kernel, are engaged with the shell or husk, since they are devoid of Gnosis to understand the kernel of religion. Though they claim that they are obedient to the Holy Book, they do not know the meaning of what they eagerly read. The bigot, being in opposition with the Lover, does not know what Love is and seeks only to go to heaven. Although they are pious, they are hypocrites. They are men of imitation, not of realization. [See also *Imitation*]
Breath	Spiritually, 'breath' refers to the Breath of the All-Merciful (*Nafas ar-Rahman*). It is the breath of the Perfect Man which revives dead hearts.
Breath of Jesus	The breath of Jesus is the breath which revives the dead. [See also *Breath*]
Candle	The candle symbolizes the Absolute Beauty of God. The Lover, falling in love with the Beloved, constantly turns around Her like a moth until his existence is annihilated by the Fire of Love.
Cavalier	Man's nafs or body is symbolised by a horse or donkey. Merged in Divine Love it becomes *Buraq* to fly to the heavens with its Cavalier, that is, Muhammad.
Cheek	Cheek symbolizes the manifestation of the lights of the self-manifestation of God.
Confirming God's Being	The phrase '*La ilaha illallah*' involves both negation and confirmation. '*La ilaha*' – 'No god' is the negation of that which is other than Allah. And, on the other hand, '*illallah*' – 'only Allah' is the confirmation of the Being of Allah.
Cup	Cup symbolizes the Heart of the Lover, thirsty for Divine Love.

Dajjal

The appearance of Dajjal is known to be one of the major signs of the end of times. In *The Feasts of Wisdom*, Niyazi Mısri, explaining the inward meaning of Dajjal, says that Dajjal's coming out is the emergence of evil attributes in the soul which hinders man from seeing divine realities.

As to the killing of Dajjal by Jesus Christ, Niyazi Mısri explains it in *The Feasts of Wisdom* as the following: "The killing of Dajjal by Christ means the annulment of the sovereignty of Dajjal. Just as Sadruddin Qunawi says: 'Dajjal is the place of manifestation of the reality of this world. It is for this reason that he is blind in the right eye, that is, he cannot perceive God. And Jesus Christ is the place of manifestation of the reality of the hereafter.'"

Dark Cloud

When the Prophet Muhammad was asked, "Where was our Lord before He created creation?" he replied, "He was in a Cloud (*A'ma*) above which and below which there is no air." Muhyiddin ibn Arabi says that this cloud is nothing other than the Breath of the All-Merciful.

Darkness

Being the opposite of light, darkness refers to nothingness or non-existence from an 'ontological' point of view; and, 'epistemologically' it refers to ignorance of what reality really is. Darkness being remoteness from the Truth, refers also to Majesty, *Jalal*. However, in another context, Darkness refers to Non-manifestation or *Ahadiyya*. [See also *Dark Cloud*]

Dawran

Dawran is a spiritual practice of the sufis in which a group of dervishes invoke God, turning in a cycle.

Day of Alast

[See *Alast*]

Divine Law

Divine Law (*Sharia*) is the outward aspect of Islam, its inner aspect being the Reality (*Haqiqa*). [See *Reality*]

Down

Down on the cheek symbolizes God's attribute of Majesty and Greatness.

Drinking

Drinking symbolizes the joy of nearness to God. [See also *Wine*]

Drop

[See *Ocean*]

Duality Duality is affirming the existence of the creation which is separate from the Existence of God, and this is nothing but *shirk*, that is, associating another existence with God.

East Wind The blowing of the East Wind symbolizes the self-manifestation of God in the creation. It is the Breath of the All-Merciful. [See also *Breath*]

Essential Name The Name 'Allah' is the Essential Name of God (*Ism-i Dhat*). But, it is not the Name of the Sheer Essence, since the Sheer Essence cannot be named or described, being beyond any description. So, the Essential Name, Allah, is the Name of the One who is qualified with the attribute of Divinity.

Eyebrows Two eyebrows indicate the opposite arcs of the circle of Being, that is, the Arc of Necessity and the Arc of Contingency, necessity and contingency being the two aspects of the Truth. And the Perfect Man, being an isthmus between them, encompasses these two aspects.

Face Face is one's essential reality. So, the Face of God denotes the Essence of God. And when God is considered as the Beloved, it also refers to Her Beauty. The self (*nafs*) or creation, being the veiling of Her Face, has to be removed to see Her Beauty.

Footstool For sufis, the Footstool (*Kursi*), a Koranic term, denotes the manifestation of the Attributes of Acts. Thus, it is where Divine tasks become manifest. What is there in the 'Throne' in potential, becoming actual, manifests in the 'Footstool'. [See also *Throne*]

Four Books The Four Books are Zaboor, the Pentateuch, the Gospel and the Koran, which were sent down to David, Moses, Jesus and Muhammad respectively. These four books refer to the four stations of understanding God. These are the unification of the Names, the unification of the Acts, unification of the Attributes, and the unification of the Essence. Therefore, the Koran represents the Essence; the Pentateuch, the self-manifestation of the Attributes; Zaboor, the self-manifestation of the Acts; and, Gospel, the self-manifestation of the Names. All of these Four Books are gathered in *Alif*, the first letter of the Arabic alphabet, which symbolizes Oneness and Essential Perfection, that is, God.

Friend	The term 'Friend' (*dost*) refers to both the Perfect Man and God.
Gnosis	Gnosis (*irfan, marifa*) is the knowledge of God's Essence and Attributes. Gnosis is a state which is achieved by witnessing (*shuhud*), that is, witnessing the Truth through the Truth which is the degree of *Haqqa'l Yaqin*. *Sharia* is like the husk of the fruit, while *Marifa* is the essence of it. The gnostics are those who are able to reach meanings from words, and realities from meanings. [See also *Reality*]
Great War	Great war is the war which is waged to defeat the greatest enemy, that is one's own self, in order to become a true Man. Muhammad, the Messenger of God, says: "The *mujahid* [that is, one who wages war] is the one who struggles against his own self in obedience to Allah."
Hair	[See *Tresses*]
Heart	The Heart where the Hidden Treasure is present is the perfect place of the self-manifestation of God.
Heaven	In the microcosmic level of human consciousness, Heaven denotes the state of being near to God. One who is in Heaven is in the presence of God's *Jamal*. [See also *Hell*]
Hell	In the microcosmic level of human consciousness, Hell is that which is surmised to be other than the Being of God. Therefore, hell is nothing but remoteness and being apart from Him. However, in reality, no one is remote from God, this being just the illusion of the unbelievers. In this sense, Hell is the presence of God's *Jalal*. [See also *Heaven*]
Hidden Treasure	The Hidden Treasure denotes the unknowable Essence of God. This term was derived from a hadith qudsi, a divinely inspired hadith, in which God declares: "I was a hidden treasure, and I wanted to be known. Hence I created the world so that I would be known." And, only the Perfect Man and the Friends of God are able to know Him, recognizing the Hidden Treasure within themselves.

Homeland According to sufis, man, on coming to this world has been separated from his origin. This is why, in this world, which is but a foreign land, sufis try to return back to their "original land" which symbolically denotes the eternal union with God.

I am the Truth "I am the Truth" (*Ana al-Haqq*) is the renowned saying of Hallaj Mansur because of which he was sentenced to death.

Jalaludin Rumi comments on the saying of Hallaj: "He said, 'I am the Truth', that is, 'I have been annihilated; the Truth remains, nothing else.' This is extreme humility and the utmost limit of servanthood. It means, 'He alone *is*.' To make a false claim and to be proud is to say, 'You are the Truth and I am the servant.' For in this way you are affirming your own existence, and duality is the necessary result. If you say, 'He is the Truth', that too is duality, for there cannot be a 'He' without an 'I'. Hence God said, 'I am the Truth.' Other than He, nothing else existed. Hallaj had been annihilated, so those were the words of God."

Ibrahim Adham While he was the Sultan of Balh, he abandoned everything he had and became a dervish. He is widely used in sufi poems as a symbol of giving up the world for the sake of God.

Imitation / God says, "I have created the world to be known,"
Realization and the Prophet Muhammad says, "He who knows himself, knows his Lord." Thus, religion is the way to attain that very knowledge of the self through which one knows the Truth. So, one has to follow the Prophet of God to attain Gnosis, he being the perfect example for humanity. In this way, one comes to realize the reality of things and the Truth, for which he has been created. But if one outwardly follows the religious orders blindly for whatever reason other than attaining that realization (*tahqiq*) of the Truth, his acts are but imitation (*taqlid*), devoid of spirit, like eating the green peel of the walnut without being aware of its kernel. [See also *Walnut*]

Jesus	Jesus symbolizes the seal of the absolute friendship of God. [See also *Dajjal*]
Jewel	Jewel (*jawhar*) denotes the meaning behind the form, and the reality of a thing behind its appearance.
Khidr	Khidr symbolizes the Perfect Guide who has drunk the Water of Life, that is who has become the perfect place of manifestation of the Essential Self-Manifestation of God.
	In sufi writings, Khidr is often mentioned in two different contexts. Firstly, he is mentioned as one who sought the Water of Life together with Alexander. According to the story, he found the Water of Life when he entered into a land of darkness.
	On the other hand, he is mentioned as the one who Moses seeks to accompany. Their story is mentioned in the Koran. [See the Koran, 18:60-82]. Many sufis like Muhyiddin ibn Arabi and Niyazi Mısri interpreted the inner meanings of the companionship between Khidr and Moses. [See also *Green Garden*]
La	'La', an Arabic word, means 'no'. [See also *Confirming God's Being*]
Land of thorns	Land of thorns symbolizes the sufferings experienced by the Lover in his strive for joining to the Beloved while in the state of separation from Her.
Last station	The last station refers to the station of *Ahadiyya*.
Letter	Existence, like words, have an outward and inward aspect, the former being the word composed of sensible letters, and the latter, the intelligible meaning that those composition of letters indicate. So letter, when used symbolically, denotes the outward existence which veils the Truth.
Lips	Lips of the Beloved denote the source of Water of Life which enlivens the soul of the Lover of God.

Love   For sufis, true Love is nothing but Divine Love. They expressed the Journey to God in terms of a lover's seeking his beloved, since there is a great similarity between them, except one is earthly and ephemeral, the other being divine and everlasting.

In the beginning of the Journey, the Lover has the bitter consciousness of being separate from the Beloved. This separation from the Beloved is the Heartache the Lover suffers; it makes everywhere a land of thorns. This Heartache can only be healed by Joining the Beloved. So, the Heartache is itself the remedy, since only with this Heartache can the Lover join his Beloved. This separation causes great grief because of which he cries and wails, that being the heartfelt invocation of the Beloved. And he risks everything, even his soul, to join his Beloved.

True Love demands from the Lover to lose himself in the Beloved. The existence of the Beloved takes so much place in the existence of the Lover that nothing remains of him. Also everything loses its value and beauty before the Beloved. This situation is symbolized by the moth burning into the candle, or a drop immersing into the ocean.

Thus through Love, through annihilation of his self or nafs, the Lover recognizes the true nature of existence and becomes a Gnostic. He sees the Beloved, God, ever-present in everything through the self-manifestation of His Names and Attributes. There is no way to recognize it without the annihilation of the self, and there can be no way to annihilate the self without Love.

Lowest Center   The Lowest Center denotes the Perfect Man, the Highest Center being the Light of Muhammad.

Mahdi   On Mahdi, Niyazi Mısri says: "The appearance of Mahdi denotes the manifestation of the Universal Intellect and Supreme Spirit, which is breathed only into the elect. And the verse, 'He breathed into him of His Spirit' [the Koran, 32:9] indicates this Supreme Spirit."

Majnun   Majnun is the love-crazed lover of Laila in the story of *Laila and Majnun*, a classic story of love, based on a semi-historical 7th century Arab story. In sufi imagery, Majnun is the one who is lost in the Love for God.

Making merry   Making merry symbolizes spiritual ardor and ecstasy, insulated from all worldly thoughts and things.

Manna and quails   Manna and quails are the two provisions sent down to the Children of Israel while they dwelt in the desert, after they left Egypt with Moses: "And We gave you the shade of clouds and sent down to you manna and quails," [the Koran, 2:57].

Mansur   Hallaj Mansur is a renown sufi who was executed because of his saying "I am the Truth". In sufi poetry, he is widely mentioned as a Martyr of Love.

Mary   Mary symbolizes the soul that receives divine inspiration, becoming heavy with Divine Light.

Mef'ulu mefa'ilun   Different forms of Arabic/Persian aruz prosody are shown by bringing together in a certain order the root words *'failatun', 'failun', 'mef'ulu', 'mefailun',* and *'fe'lun'* which have no meaning in themselves. *"Mef'ulu mefa'ilun mef'ulu mefa'ilun"* and *"Failatun failatun failun"* are two of the most common prosody forms.

Middle Circle   The Middle Circle denotes the Muhammadan Community, referring its being temperate and balanced, avoiding extremities.

Mole   Black mole, or beauty-spot symbolizes the indivisible Oneness of God.

Most Holy Effusion   The Most Holy Effusion (*Fayd-i-Aqdas*) is the Self-Manifestation of the Essence, through which the immutable essences of all the creation has become manifest in the Divine Knowledge.

Moth   [See *candle*]

Mustafa   Mustafa is a title of the Prophet Muhammad which means 'chosen' or 'elect'.

Night Journey The night Journey is the Prophet Muhammad's ascension into the presence of God.

Night of Ascent The night in which the Prophet Muhammad ascended into the presence of God.

Night of Power Night of Power (*Laila-i-Qadr*) is a very blessed night within the month of Ramadan, about which the Koran says: "We have sent it down on the Night of Power. And do you know what the Night of Power is? The Night of Power is better than a thousand months. The angels and the Spirit descend therein, by the permission of their Lord, on every task. Peace it is until the coming of dawn." [The Koran, 97]

Nightingale The nightingale symbolizes the Lover of God.

Ocean Ocean stands for the Unity of God, the only Being beyond the shadow reality of the universe. The drop is the false consciousness of the self, surmising that it has a separate existence in itself, an existence other than God — but, when it merges into the Ocean, it becomes unified with it.

On the other hand, while the Ocean represents the Absolute Being of God, the waves of the Ocean stand for the becoming of the world of manifoldness which has no existence in itself, being only the self-manifestation of the Absolute Being.

Other The phrase 'that which is other' refers to everything other than God.

Party of Salvation This term is derived from the following hadith of the Prophet Muhammad: "My community will be divided into seventy-three sects all of which, save one will go to Hell." The Companions asked: "O Messenger of God, which is the sect that will go to Paradise?" He said: "That one which stuck to the path on which I and my Companions are."

Pearl The pearl symbolizes divine knowledge. In this symbolism, gnostics are symbolized as being divers who harvest pearls in the depths of the ocean. Pearl may also symbolize the Perfect Man, the man who has spiritually realized himself. [See also *Pearl bed*]

Pearl bed

While in traditional poetry, the mouth is the bed of pearls, that is, the beautiful teeth of the beloved, in sufi poetry, it is the source of divine knowledge. [See also *Pearl*]

Perfect Man

Universe is but the manifestation of the Names/Attributes of God, which are manifested dispersedly throughout the Universe. Within creation, only man can be the locus of manifestation of all the Names/Attributes of God, gathering together them in his being, as it is indicated in the verse, "And He taught Adam all the Names," [the Koran, 2:31]. So, man is a mirror for God through whom He contemplates His own Beauty. However, in order for all the Names of God to be manifested from himself, man has to annihilate himself in God and subsist with Him, becoming a Perfect Man.

Place where two seas meet

In the Koran, it is said: "God let forth the two seas that meet together, between them an isthmus that they do not overpass," [the Koran, 55:20]. Niyazi Mısri expounds the meaning of this verse in *The Feasts of Wisdom*: "What is intended by two seas is *Sharia* and *Haqiqa*. Every knowledge and deed in *Sharia* is also found in *Haqiqa*. But according with God's wisdom and power, there is an isthmus between them which prevents them from mingling. If these two seas, that is, *Sharia* and *Haqiqa*, or the outward knowledge and inward knowledge meet, one becomes 'the place where two seas meet.' And Moses found Khidr there."

'The place where two seas meet' is also conceived as the isthmus between the Ocean of Necessity and that of Contingency.

Polo stick

The polo stick symbolizes the Universal Will of God, while the ball symbolizes the perfect servant who abandons his own individual will before the Will of God.

Poor

This term has a special meaning in sufism. It is often used as a synonym for the sufi or dervish. [See also *Poverty*]

Poverty	The meaning of poverty is explained in the Koran: "O mankind! You are poor in your relation to God, while God is He Who is the All-Wealthy and Worthy of Praise" [35:15]. The Prophet Muhammad, being the Perfect Man, states how he conceives of the essential poverty of his being human: "*Al-faqru fakhri* — Poverty is my glory."
	One who is perfectly conscious of one's essential poverty before God and one's absolute dependence on Him gets rid of his illusory self, and as he sees that the One that acts in himself is God, he becomes Rich with God.
Praise of the Universe	This phrase denotes the Prophet Muhammad for whom the universe has been created.
Prostration	Prostration alludes to obedience and submission through respect and humility. In the Koran, it is indicated that one has to prostrate oneself before Adam, that is, the Perfect Man who is the perfect place of manifestation of God. [See the Koran, 15:29-31]
Qaf	[See *Anqa*]
Quarry	The quarry symbolizes Love, while the hunter symbolizes the Lover.
Qul Hu wallah	"Say: He is Allah ..." This is the beginning of the Sura of Ikhlas. [See the Koran, 112]
Reality	In sufi context, Reality (*Haqiqa*) refers to the inward essential truth. The sufis seek after knowing God through self-knowledge, which has four levels in itself: *Sharia*, *Tariqa*, *Haqiqa* and *Marifa*.
Relativities	Relativities (*izafat*) are the apparent forms in opposition to the inward realities.
Retreat	Retreat (*khalwa*) is a sufi practice in which a disciple isolates himself for forty days under the guidance of a spiritual master in order to be able to purify himself from worldly ties.
Rose	Rose symbolizes the Beloved.
Rose garden	Rose garden symbolizes the Oneness of God.

Sama   *Sama* is the the spiritual dance of the dervishes; it's dhikr, accompanied by music and whirling.

Samma wajhullah "[Wherever you turn,] there is the Face of Allah." [The Koran, 2:115]

Satan   When Adam was created, God commanded Satan and all the other angels to prostrate themselves before Adam. Satan, not being able to apprehend the inward meaning of Adam, refused to bow down to him. He reasoned to himself that he was superior to Adam since he was made of fire while Adam was only made of clay. In this one act of defiance, he introduced the sins of pride, envy, and disobedience into the world. When confronted by God, he refused to take any responsibility for his sins; instead he accused God of leading him astray.

Seal of all the   Seal of all the Messengers is the Prophet Muham-
Messengers   mad, being the last Prophet.

Secret   *Secret* (*sirr*) denotes the innermost meaning or hidden wisdom; it's the center of spiritual consciousness of man. The relation of the spirit to the body is the same as the relation of the Secret to the Heart. Whereas the Heart is the place of Gnosis, the Secret is the place of Witnessing.

Secret of   The reality of contingent things which were unman-
Eternity   ifest in the eternal knowledge of God, wanted Him to manifest themselves. So they came into existence, becoming manifest according with their aptitude. This is called the secret of eternity.

Separation   Separation (*tafsil*) is the opposite of union (*jam*). [See also *Union*]

Seven Reciters   *Qurra-i Seba.* Seven notable reciters of the Koran who established the subtelties of reciting It. When used in a symbolic way, it may allude to the seven inner meanings of the Koran.

Shoreless   The Shoreless Ocean denotes the Absolute Being of
Ocean   God.

Sidra *Sidrat-ul-Muntaha* is the Lote Tree of the Furthest Limit. This tree is mentioned in the Koran. [See the Koran 53:14]

Soberness Soberness denotes the state of stability (*tamkeen*) that the seeker experiences at the very end of his inner journey as he has passed beyond the state of alternation (*talween*) in which he undergoes constantly altering inner states. Especially, those who are intoxicated by Divine Love are considered as men of alteration.

Speech of Birds Speech of Birds denotes the Language of Meaning. This is indicated in the Koran: "Solomon was David's heir. He said: "O you people! We have been taught the speech of birds" [27:16].

Strand The strands of the Beloved symbolizes the Divine Beauty or the manifestations of God.

Subsistence The Station of Subsistence, *Baqabillah*, which comes after Annihilation, *Fanafillah*, is the station of the Perfect Man. This is a degree in which the Absolute Essence manifests Himself in a perfect place of manifestation. In this station, the Perfect Man witnesses the Truth in creation and creation in the Truth without either being a hindrance of the other, that being the perfect witnessing. [See also *Annihilation*]

Sugar Sugar symbolizes Gnosis.

Sun Being the source of light, the Sun symbolizes God. [See *Light*].

Supreme Name The Supreme Name (*Ism-i Azam*) is the Name which encompasses all the Divine Names. So, it denotes the name 'Allah'.

Tavern The tavern is the heart of the Perfect Guide; being the treasury of Divine Love. It also means the place where dervishes, the Lovers of God, stay in the presence of the Guide.

Three kingdoms of nature The three kingdoms of nature are the bodies of minerals, plants and animals.

Throne   The Throne (*Arsh*) is the Highest Heaven that includes
all the worlds, spiritual or material, on which "the
Merciful is established," [the Koran, 20:5]. In man,
being a microcosmos, the Throne corresponds to the
Heart. So in its true meaning the Throne is the Heart
of the Perfect Man. "Neither My heaven nor My earth
could contain Me, but the soft, humble heart of My
believing servant can contain Me," indicates it. As the
Throne is the highest point of the universe, the earth
(*farsh*) is the lowest point. [See also *Kursi*]

Tooba   Tooba is mentioned in the Koran as a tree in the
Heaven.

Tresses   Tresses refer both to the unknown, unattainable Ipseity
and to the veil of *Jalal*, that is the whole creation which
veils the Beauty of God. So, tresses symbolize the mani-
foldness veiling Oneness. In this sense, being bewitched
by dark tresses implies ignorance and unbelief.

Trial   Trial (*kahr*) is unpleasant situations one may experi-
ence as the manifestation of God's *Jalal*. On the other
hand, its opposite, favour (*lutf*), is the manifestation
of God's *Jamal*.

Trust   God says in the Koran: "We did indeed offer the Trust
to the Heavens and the Earth and the Mountains;
but they refused to undertake it, being afraid thereof:
but man undertook it; he was indeed tyrannous and
ignorant," [the Koran, 33:72]. Abd al-Karim al-Jili
comments on the verse in *The Perfect Man*: "What is
intended by the Trust in this verse is but the Truth
with respect to His Essence, Names and Attributes.
There is no one who can undertake this Trust with
his all existence in existence except the Perfect Man."
And he continues, saying that man is tyrant since he
tyrannizes his self, not knowing its true value. And he
is ignorant, not knowing the high degree of his self.

Truth of   Truth of certainty (*Haqq al-yaqin*) is the last of the
certainty three degrees of knowledge mentioned in the Koran.
Ilm al-yaqin belongs to those having discursive reason-
ing; *Ayn al-yaqin*, to those having knowledge through
tasting and unveiling; and, *Haqq al-yaqin*, to those who
attained Gnosis. In the truth of certainty the knower
and the known becomes unified. [See also *Gnosis*]

Two bows' length or even nearer	*"Qaba qawsaini aw adna,"* [the Koran, 53:9]. "Two bows' length" refers to the station of Union of Union (*jamu'l jam*), and "– even nearer" refers to the station of *Ahadiyya*.
Union	On union, Niyazi Mısri says in *The Feasts of Wisdom*: "O friend, while inwardly you should try to join with God, outwardly you should know your separation. That is, inwardly you should be on the side of union (*jam*), and outwardly you should be on the side of separation (*farq*). You should not be veiled from Oneness by multiplicity and from multiplicity by Oneness. You should reconcile servanthood and gnosis so as to free yourself from dangers."
Water of Life	Water of Life denotes the Essential self-manifestation of God.
Wave	While the Ocean is the Oneness of God, the waves are the self-manifestations of God, manifesting themselves through the world of manifoldness. [See also *Ocean*]
Whim	Whim (*hawa*) is the inclination of the self to the ephemeral things to satisfy his worldly desires. So, it is what hinders man from inclining towards God.
Wine	Wine is symbolic of the Gnosis of God, the outcome of which is Divine Love.
Witnessing	Witnessing (*shahada, mushahada*) is God's being present in the Heart. It's the degree of the Truth of Certainty. [See also *Truth of Certainty*]
Yunus	Yunus Emre, the well-known Anatolian Turkish sufi poet of the 14th century.
Zulkarnain	Literally, Zulkarnain means 'Of two Horns', symbolizing connection (*tashbih*) and disconnection (*tanzih*).

REFERENCES TO KORANIC AND PROPHETIC SAYINGS

Below are listed the Koranic verses and Prophetic sayings that are directly mentioned or alluded to in the poems by Niyazi Mısri.

The Koranic Verses

- "And He taught Adam all the Names," [the Koran, 2:31].
- "And We gave you the shade of clouds and sent down to you manna and quails..." [the Koran, 2:57].
- "*Samma wajhullah*" — "[Wherever you turn,] there is the Face of Allah," [the Koran, 2:115].
- "Allah! There is no God save Him, the Alive, the Eternal. Neither slumber nor sleep overtakes Him. Unto Him belongs whatsoever is in the heavens and whatsoever is in the earth. Who is he that intercedes with Him save by His leave? He knows that which is in front of them and that which is behind them, while they encompass nothing of His knowledge save what He will. His Footstool includes the heavens and the earth, and He is never weary of preserving them. He is the Sublime, the Tremendous," [the Koran, 2:255].

- "Everyday He is upon some task," [the Koran, 5:29].
- "'When I have fashioned him and breathed into him of My spirit, fall ye down in obeisance unto him.' So the angels prostrated themselves, all of them together: Not so Iblis: he refused to be among those who prostrated themselves," [the Koran, 15:29-31].
- "He fashioned him and breathed into him of His Spirit," [the Koran, 32:9].
- "We offered the Trust unto the heavens and the earth and the hills, but they shrank from bearing it and were afraid of it. And man assumed it," [the Koran, 33:72].
- "And you will see the angels surrounding the Throne on all sides, singing glory and praise to their Lord," [the Koran, 39:75].
- "Two bows' length or even nearer," [the Koran, 53:9].
- "Say: He is Allah, the One and Only; Allah, the Eternal, Absolute; He begetteth not, nor is He begotten; and there is none like unto Him," [the Koran, 112].

The Divinely Inspired Traditions (Hadith Qudsi)

- "If it weren't for you, [I would have not created the worlds]."
- "I am not contained in the heavens and earth, but I am contained in the heart of the believer."
- "I was a hidden treasure and I wanted to be known, so I created the creation so that I would be known."

The Prophetic Sayings

- "Poverty is my glory."
- "He who knows himself, [knows his Lord]."